Methods of MADNESS

Methods of MADNESS

100 Writers Discuss Their Craft

Edited by
Andy Rausch,
Becky Narron, and
T. Fox Dunham

BearManor Media
2020

Methods of Madness: 100 Writers Discuss Their Craft

© 2020 Andy Rausch, Becky Narron, and T. Fox Dunham

All rights reserved.

No portion of this publication may be reproduced, stored, and/or copied electronically (except for academic use as a source), nor transmitted in any form or by any means without the prior written permission of the publisher and/or author.

Published in the United States of America by:

BearManor Media
1317 Edgewater Dr. #110
Orlando, FL 32804

BearManorMedia.com

Printed in the United States.

Typesetting and layout by John Teehan

ISBN—978-1-62933-524-7

Table of Contents

Introduction: "Writers Are Full of Shit" 1

1. Finding the Muse, or Where Do You Get Your Ideas? 3

2. The Writing Process 37

3. Editing and Rewriting 71

4. Advice For Aspiring Writers 105

Writers Are Full of Shit
by Andy Rausch

WILLIAM GOLDMAN, one of the greatest writers who ever lived, once said, "Nobody knows anything." And it's true. You know the old adage that opinions are like assholes and that everyone's got one? The same is true with writing advice. There is no singular path to write properly. What works for one writer won't work for thirty others. For instance, some writers like Stephen King write while blasting heavy metal music. That absolutely won't work for me. I need silence. Ultra-silence. (The sound of a TV in the next room will drive me mad.) So for me, raucous music is a no-go. But it obviously works for King, who is one of the most gifted wordsmiths ever to put words to page. So when a writer gives you advice, you must take it with a grain of salt. You have to find your own way. Despite their successes, what works for James Patterson or J.K. Rowling may not work for you. To this you might ask, "Then why did you publish this book, and why should I read it?"

This book is primarily for the novice. The would-be, wannabe, hope-to-be-one-day writer. Every writer in this book was sitting where you are once. A writer must learn what does and doesn't work for him or her. As such, it's helpful to learn what works for others and why that is, as well as what doesn't. These tidbits may not help you, but they very well may. You have to discover and then fine-tune your own methods, often through process of elimination. And you have to know what the methods are in order to try them and find out if they work for you. Many won't, but chances are good that at least a few will.

After several decades of writing (and two being paid to do so), I find that my own process is constantly evolving. What works for me on one book may not on another. So even now, with nearly forty books published, it's important for me to be aware of alternate methods. Writing is a strange beast. It's also very personal. In a way, it's spiritual in that it's just between you and your muse (whatever "muse" means to you).

In a book of this nature, it's important to recognize upfront that there will be copious redundancies here. A lot of writers give some of the same advice. In my mind, those that pop up frequently are the most important to consider. If many published authors are saying the same things, they're likely saying them for good reason. Even then, each writer offers that piece of advice in a unique manner, and sometimes there are lessons to be learned within the individual nuances.

But again, it's important to remember that every writer has to find his or her own way. No matter how many methods and techniques they're presented with, there is no sure-fire road to become a better writer and/or becoming a successful one. So when any writer—myself included—says "this is the only way," they're full of shit. My hope is that one day you will be a success yourself, whatever success means to you. (For one writer it's getting published, and for another it's selling lots of books.) And then, once you've accomplished this, you too can be full of shit. But until that day, it's important to study the craft and, most of all, write, write, write.

Finding the Muse, Or, Where Do You Get Your Ideas?

STEWART O'NAN (*Snow Angels*): The only easy answers come after the fact, so I distrust them. I'm curious about people in certain predicaments, and about certain charged settings, but often my plans to write about them fall through after months or years of work. Why do some projects last and others don't? If I knew, I wouldn't waste so much time and effort pursuing so many false starts and dead ends.

MICHELLE BOWSER (*A Gross Miscellany*): My ideas come from the crazy world around me. It could be anything at any given time or place. I tend to notice the absurdity in everyday life.

ANDY RAUSCH (*Bloody Sheets*): I get a lot of ideas from the things I read or the movies I watch. I don't rip them off, but if I really let my mind go, the scenarios presented will lead me to consider different things or ways those situations could go, which often leads to completely new ideas.

MARK SLADE (*A Six Gun & the Queen of Light*): Usually the past. Either events in history or in old films or TV. Sometimes it's what people say in conversation. I remember one incident where a friend at work said he knew a guy who accidentally robbed his mother's house. Another time, I misheard a customer say she left her purse in the last century. Both ideas were used in stories.

When I'm uninspired, a cup of coffee sometimes gets me going. I've also laid down and drifted to sleep when I had story problems and wake up quickly to have the story fully realized.

GARY VINCENT (*Darkened Hills*): I enjoy writing about things that interest me. I really don't like boring stuff, so my inspiration tends to drift to the edges of realistic fantasy. Often times, my writing is a bit dark. I'm moody and sarcastic and exercise that side of my persona when writing. But I also have a very warped sense of humor and try to incorporate the absurd comedic element to even the darkest of my writings. The thing that gets me going at the start of a project is typically just the gratification of getting one of the millions of thoughts running through my mind out on paper. Sometimes I develop a complete treatment or outline for a story before I get into the weeds, and then when I'm feeling challenged, I can look back at the treatment and see where the story should be heading and make adjustments accordingly.

BECKY NARRON (short-story writer, numerous anthologies): Most of my ideas come from dreams or parts of dreams I've had. I dream in vivid color. Trust me, it isn't a good thing. Nightmares. Most nights, I'm afraid to try to sleep. Anyone that knows me knows I never sleep.

JOE R. LANSDALE (*Bubba Ho-Tep*): I always like to challenge myself, and sometimes I manage it more than others, but I'm inspired by so many things. Partly because I have a lot of interest as a reader and as a person. I am my muse, as we all are, and I learned long ago to pay attention to my subconscious, that's where I find my stories. We have all manner of material there, and we have to teach ourselves to listen to it.

CHRIS ROY (*Her Name Is Mercie*): [Note: Chris, a published author, is serving a life sentence in prison.] Earlier this year, I was on the yard working out with a couple guys when an insane conversation gave me a great story idea. One guy was joking about escaping and starving and having to eat shit or drink piss. I said, "You can drink your piss, and it won't hurt you. But you are better off cutting off a little sliver of meat from your leg to eat than choking down a turd." We laughed and kept exercising, and the joke turned into a scene in my head, a story forming around it. Back in my cell, I started making notes for one of my darkest stories, "Hunger." That's how a lot of my story ideas form, bantering with guys or while saying something incredibly stupid to a girl just to get her to giggle.

    The bigger the challenge, the more I'm motivated. If I feel something is too easy, I'm in no hurry to get it done. It's always been like that, and writing is no different.

GRAHAM MASTERSON (*The Manitou*): I was trained from the age of 17 as a newspaper reporter and then became the editor of two men's magazines, *Mayfair* and *Penthouse*. Those jobs taught me to see stories where other people often couldn't and to mix two stories together to make one dramatic novel. In my first horror novel, *The Manitou*, for example, I was inspired by the pregnancy of my wife Wiescka and a story I remembered about Native American spirits I had read in *The Buffalo Bill Annual* when I was a boy. Hence, a 300-year-old Native American medicine man is reborn in the present day to take his revenge on the white man. I have used the same device several times, bringing back to life legendary demons from various ethnic folk-tales and seeing how today's ordinary people would deal with them.

I read the Irish newspapers every day, and they give me ideas for the series of crime thrillers I am writing about Detective Superintendent Katie Maguire, which is set in Cork, where Wiescka and I lived for five years. So I never get stuck for ideas. In fact, I have more ideas for novels than I will ever be able to write about in my lifetime.

ELKA RAY (*Saigon Dark*): Every now and then, a manuscript I've invested months or even years in goes belly up and I decide to quit writing. I last about a week and then a new story grabs me. The characters become background noise. I start to think: "What's next? What if this happened?" Ideas won't let go. Resistance is futile.

EDDIE GENEROUS (*Radio Run*): It doesn't really work that way for me. I think after I opened myself up to penning that first idea, my brain became like a fishing net, but a shitty one at first. The more ideas I accepted, the more my net caught. Used to be, I tried to write a story for every idea, but I've come to learn that not everything is worth saving, so I let the fish go and if they keep getting caught in my net, then I know they're keepers, and I have to explore them. Now that I've explored so many ideas, good and bad, my net is constantly functioning while I'm reading, watching TV, taking walks, eating Mickey D's, dropping my recycling off, whatever. I'm picking up little things and big things. I guess to keep on the fish, some of those little things feed into a bigger fish, and once there's enough there, I have to get busy.

As for what gets me started, quite often I've planned a date that I'm going to get on with one of the lingering ideas, but then I get in a grouch, and the afternoon is quiet or something and before I know it, a few thousand words are there, and the idea is blooming. As for getting stuck, it doesn't happen very often, because I don't plot. When it does happen, I backtrack to a fork in the story and delete, take a right instead of a left, or I set the story aside (usually indefinitely). Sometimes I still tackle stinky fish.

BRIAN BARR (*Dark Ripple: When Lovecraft Met Crowley*): Dreams and research are a huge influence for my writing. When it comes to dreams, I have ideas that hit me out of nowhere, sometimes as nearly complete stories that just need a few details ironed out here and there. That's how my 3 Hs Trilogy came about, along with certain scenes in my *Carolina Daemonic* series and other books. As far as research, I've always loved learning about history, different cultures, philosophy, science, and other topics which have helped me come up with concepts for stories as well.

JOHN W. WOOD (*White Crow*): History is my inspiration. I was brought up around books and the collection of antiques by my parents. Both of my parents were writers; my mother wrote books, my father music. I had an excellent history teacher in high school who also inspired me. When I read something, say about the Civil War, I can envision the sounds of harness and iron-rimmed wheels. I know the smell of burnt powder, the shouting of orders, the chaos of the military from experience. Then I wonder what a man would feel at a time when he knows he may die. For me, it's only a short step away from a conversation with that man. Where are you from, who was your family, what makes you unique, are you a hero or a coward? As I write, I often Google questions about the times I'm writing about, like words used in that era, clothing. Soon that man has a name, and he's meeting people, and they talk, and I have 80,000 words and a novel.

G. MIKI HAYDEN (*Strings*): How do I limit the ideas to the ones that will bear viable fruit is the question. As humans, we are idea machines—ideas pop up minute to minute. We have to screen the auditioning ideas with our knowledge of what markets might be looking for, ideas with legs, ideas that have at least an internal logic.

The one time in my writing where I was feeling challenged was in writing *Question Woman & Howling Sky*—which finally made it into print. I had them in the desert, and where do I go from here? Well, the characters were in a dilemma themselves, so I sent them wandering around the desert while I grasped at straws. *Aha!* The idea popped up, and the book is at Amazon.

JENNIFER BROWN (*Hate List*): Inspiration is a bugger to explain, partly because no one thing has ever inspired me to write a story (it's always a combination of things—a little "perfect storm" in my right brain) and also because sometimes (okay, most of the time) the ideas truly come from nowhere. Or everywhere. Or anywhere. See? This is what I mean by bugger. I used to think this was a divine "gift" aspect of writing—and maybe it is—but now I really think it's just a trained subconscious. I absorb little details as I'm moving frenetically and completely unaware throughout my day, and at moments when my mind is quiet and empty, those details are able to wriggle to the forefront. Sometimes I know what sparked that wriggly little detail—a news story or a podcast or an overheard conversation or just something from my own past—and sometimes I don't. And honestly, most of the time, I'm not concerned with where the story idea came from; I'm just wanting to get it on paper before it goes away.

Not to sound even more enigmatic, but when it comes to beginning a project, I wait for the characters to start talking to me. When I can't get the story out of my mind, I'm interested. When I hear my main characters' voices, I'm very interested. When I find myself researching, I'm on the verge of committing. When I hear that first sentence in my mind's ear loud and clear, I'm going for it. My gut knows when a story is the right story to pursue. I just have to be patient, which is sometimes a challenge. New ideas are exciting!

What keeps me going when I feel challenged is my mantra: *The rough draft is where the story happens; revisions are where the magic happens.* So if it's feeling off or clunky or draggy or whatever negative during the first draft, I don't sweat it. I only write forward until I reach THE END, and know that when I go back through it, I will add things that bring the magic. And I know I will remove those clunky, draggy, whatever negative parts at that time. To me, writing is always a fluid process, and perfection is never reached (I mean, it really can't be reached with something as subjective as story). If I picked up one of my published books from five years, eight years, ten years ago, I would still find things to change, to manipulate, to hone, to cut, to add. It's kind of an exciting process, really, because when you think of the story in those terms—as a moving, evolving entity—it makes the story more a part of its own creation process. It's…alive!

DAVID CLARK (*Game Master*): Usually it is a single scene, gag, or concept that comes to me from something in real life. As an example, one of my books was inspired by walking past a large-sized version of the Connect Four game in the lobby where I work. It was there as part of a tail-gating display for an upcoming playoff game. I passed it on the way to lunch and between the time I saw it, fixed a salad in the café, and walked back to my desk. I had the entire book constructed in my head. I find that the stories I have always connected with the best as a reader are those that are somewhat based on something real. That always grabbed my attention, so as a writer, I take that connection the reader develops and send them on twists and turns any roller coaster would be jealous of.

I am motivated by seeing where the story goes. Most of the time, I only write with a rough chapter outline. The story grows organically, and that is where my motivation comes from. I enjoy seeing how the characters develop and interact with each other and how the story develops. I know the beginning and the end, but the journey in between is as enjoyable to me as I hope it is to the reader.

SAMANTHA BRYANT (*Face the Change: Menopausal Superheroes*): Many of my ideas stem from something I'm annoyed or upset by. This probably started in my childhood with the strongly-worded letters I would leave for my parents when they were being unfair and insisting that I go to bed at a child's bedtime or pick up the stack of books that had fallen over and nearly tripped my mother when she tried to put away my socks. Clearly, they didn't understand that a genius of my status needed long hours of quiet with books and music to fuel her creativity and this did not leave time for chores or excessive sleeping.

Sometimes I don't know I'm upset about something until I recognize it after the fact in my writing. I remember finishing my first novel (a hot mess of a thing that we'll call a practice run) and beginning to read it through for edits, and only then realizing that I was writing the dynamic of my first marriage. Apparently, I wasn't done processing that yet.

The *Menopausal Superhero* series was definitely about things that scare and upset me. Getting older is not for sissies, and as a lifelong superhero and comic book fan, I was pretty fed up with everyone being somewhere between sixteen and twenty-five, gorgeous, and perfectly fit. I started to wonder what it would be like if the person who got superpowers hated it because it screwed with their well-laid plans and carefully-organized lives. Besides, the X-Men taught us that with great hormones, come superpowers! I didn't get mine the first go-round, so I figure menopause is my second chance.

Of course, anger and outrage can only take you so far. When a project starts to founder, it usually helps me to map out what I've already written and make a list of the questions I've left unanswered. Generally, one of them will spark my imagination and get me flowing again. I also find it helpful to revisit the initial spark. Why was I writing this in the first place instead of one of the other seventeen ideas tapping on my shoulder for attention? What made me pick it to give such long hours of focus to? Remembering why I loved the idea or what held me about it lets me fall into again.

CHRIS MILLER (*A Murder of Saints*): There are any number of things which inspire me. Most of the time, I don't have a problem getting the juices flowing, especially when inspiration strikes. Most of the inspiration comes from either real-life events, something in the news, or it comes from other works, books, and movies, where elements of several things come together to become something all its own. My current work in progress, as a matter of fact, was inspired by some real-life events in my own life, and from both *It* by Stephen King and the Netflix series *Stranger Things*. I'd just re-read the book, and saw the first season of that show, and things started percolating. Before I knew it, some real-world things came into the mix, and I was away and writing something that's wholly original and its own, but inspired by these other things. It's when things like this come together that the muse really gets tickled, and she starts pouring out ideas and scenes in vivid detail. It's a wonderful thing when that happens.

MAX ALLAN COLLINS (*Road to Peridition*): I write for a living. I do not have the luxury of waiting for a muse to tap me on the shoulder. But I am always thinking about story, and story possibilities—things that happen in my life, things going on in the news. I do occasionally react to stories by others, stories I particularly like—my novel and indie film *Mommy* was a reversal of *The Bad Seed*: what if the perfect mother was the sociopath, and it was her little girl who came to that realization? What if the wandering samurai pushing his kid in a baby cart, looking for revenge, was a thirties' gangster with an adolescent son accompanying him on a similar quest? Doing as much historical fiction as I do, I'm always on the lookout for interesting material. The *Lone Wolf and Cub* influence on *Road to Perdition* included research I'd done on a real-life Rock Island mob boss, John Looney, who had a psycho son and who had betrayed a loyal lieutenant. I make those kinds of connections all the time. *Perdition* also included my being "into" Hong Kong crime films of the time, specifically director John Woo.

THOMAS GUNTHER (*The Big Book of Bootleg Horror: Volume Four*): Inspiration comes from everywhere. I might be watching TV, a movie, reading, or listening to the radio. Typically, story ideas come to me when I'm not looking for them—usually at work or when I'm in the shower. Normally, my mind will be quiet, receptive. However, I could have a mind full of worry and agitations and suddenly have an idea pop into my head in the middle of it all. Once I wrote a story based on a nap-mare.

I'm usually stoked about a new story idea, but I have far more story ideas than I actually have stories. I have files full of unfinished stories and some finished stories. The finished ones are those that held my attention, or I should say, allowed me to stay focused in a singular sense. I originally wanted to write fantasy (which I may still do in the future). Nine times out of ten, though, I would overwhelm myself with details, leading me off on tangents that would prove counterproductive. But anytime I have a new idea I try to get it on paper, regardless. That way, if I lose focus, I can return to it in the future.

On the other paw, if I'm working on something for a themed anthology with an approaching deadline, then I have to work through a challenge. And I'm not always able to do that. I have to want it badly enough—then I always find a way.

JOHN PALISANO (*Night of 1,000 Beasts*): So many of my favorite works began as dreams. I've had awful dreams since I was a kid. One of my therapists recommended writing them out to cope. It helped. But many elements from them have turned into stories or novels. I still draw from them extensively. I also do a lot of free drawing and play music, especially if I get stuck. That usually helps.

MAXWELL BAUMAN (*The Anarchist Kosher Cookbook*): When I'm looking for ideas, I like to think about a theme and how it may have been used in fiction or history. Then I look at how I can transpose it into something new, and that can be something as simple as changing the style, the location, or the sequence. Once I have these things in mind, I turn my attention to the characters and start asking the hard questions of who these people are, what they want, and how they'll change by the end of the story. Before I start writing the first draft, I develop a ten-point outline, each plot point just a sentence long, so I can see the full story from beginning to end. Potential challenges to the story can be spotted sooner. It's easier to fix plot holes when they're just a few lines long, instead of having to scrap full pages.

BEV VINCENT (*Flight or Fright*): Ideas are never a problem. Ideas are everywhere. The air is full of ideas. The issue for me is taking ideas and turning them into stories. Usually this requires at least two ideas that may seem unrelated, but which mesh together in an unusual way. But that still isn't enough to get started. Before putting pen to paper, I have to have a character or a set of characters and at least a surface-level understanding of what they want. Once I have all those things, I can begin a story. Much may change during the writing phase, which is a journey of discovery, but if I try to start sooner, I may find myself spinning wheels and getting nowhere. Pushing the string instead of pulling it, as I've heard it described elsewhere.

One of the nice things about my writing spectrum is that I always have several things either going at once or stacked up. If I'm having trouble with one project—generally fiction—then I can move on to an essay or an interview or a book review. nonfiction is easier for me, so I can get something done during my limited writing time and not feel like I've wasted it.

If I'm stuck on a story, I'll step away and do something relatively mindless. I used to go for long bike rides, when I could let my mind drift. These days, I get on our elliptical trainer and burn some calories while I contemplate the story I'm working on. Sometimes I get so involved in story rumination while I'm in the shower that I can't remember whether I've washed my hair yet or not. When I go to sleep at night, if I'm working on a story, I may go back to the beginning in my mind and tell it to myself in the hopes that I'll get a little farther with it, either before I go to sleep or after.

Occasionally, I do something deliberate to help feed the creative beast. For example, I'm currently taking part in a Citizen's Police Academy run by our sheriff's office. Each week, there are presentations by the different groups within that organization: gang detail, SWAT, forensics, organized crime, dispatch, etc. It's all grist for the mill, and something may come out of it someday in an unexpected manner.

PAUL D. BRAZILL (*Cold London Blues*): It's usually a phrase or a slice of dialogue that comes to mind. Sometimes a person I remember meeting. Usually something odd, askew, and hopefully funny!

TRAVIS WALLACE (*Clues*): My primary muse is my outlet to what is taking place around me, be it on a world/society level or on a personal/family level. I am a diagnosed depressive, and I internalize a lot of what takes place around me. Writing is my outlet to get my initial, often irrational, thoughts and feelings down, and then I open the door to what would take place if there was no moral code or legal boundaries to how I would approach this situation. Take the filter off. This happens easier when I am stressed or the dark cloud starts to move in on me.

Having a primary muse means there is also a secondary muse, and this is where I guide my characters' tone or approach. If it is more of an emotional time, my muse is nature. The wind, trees, crisp air—all of this talks to me. I literally hear the words being spoken to me, and I am taking notes as fast as I can. If the time calls for a darker approach or the times when I say fuck moral or ethics, I tend to drink. Wine or scotch gets me there, and then the next day, I usually read what I have put down and wonder who spoke to me.

PAUL HEATLEY (*An Eye for an Eye*): I guess I'm a proactive writer, because I feel what keeps me going, what inspires me and what brings new ideas, is writing. If I'm writing, if I maintain a regular schedule, ideas come, inspiration comes, more than I can handle, so I'm scribbling constantly in notebooks, on scraps of paper, just trying to get it all down so I won't forget. Writing itself is my muse.

BRIAN JAMES LANE (*Fright Feast*): My muse is being abnormal. I see things differently. I imagine what could have happened differently in an otherwise normal situation. This often leads me down a rabbit hole. There are many interesting turns going down that mental abyss. If they are thought-provoking enough, I jot them down in an idea bank. This is literally a stream-of-consciousness document that poses the "what if" question over and over again. Then, later I go back and revisit the repository to see if any of those "what ifs" would make a good story. If so, I develop them. Expand on them. If not, they die in that graveyard of ideas. I have many more burial plots than stories. It is more of a shotgun approach to creativity, but it helps the flow to continue.

If I am stuck, then I impose limitations on myself. I create barriers which help to reform thoughts in such a fashion as to bolster creativity. For example, what if I could only write a story in only 365 words? What if I took this situation and set it in 1986 instead of today? What if I made the antagonist a female rather than a male? What if I killed off this character and kept that one alive instead? Strangely enough, thinking inside a box helps me to get out of one.

CARMEN AMATO (*Cliff Diver*): I write mystery and suspense, with a crime fiction edge. At the beginning of a project, I'll have a concept based on a true crime and plan for certain relationships to develop or devolve. Then it's on to the outline phase using sticky notes. When I feel challenged, I grab a sticky off the outline and write out a scene longhand.

PAUL TREMBLAY (*Head Full of Ghosts*): I like to imagine myself as a magpie writer. I have no idea if the following metaphor is true to that particular bird, but work with me: I build my nests by taking bits of grass, straw, candy bar wrappers, and other weird bits, and eventually, it does look like a nest and not just a collection of random junk. (So, I build my stories with ideas from all kinds of sources including but not limited to what I read, what I watch, what I listen to). I generally embrace influence, and the hope is even though my nests (um, stories) are comprised of riffs on other folks' ideas, that the final product will be uniquely mine.

At the start of a project, I scratch out some ideas/notes in a notebook and kick the idea(s) around there for a while. Often the nest (um, story) collapses there in the notebook. But sometimes it doesn't, and it grows from there.

LILY LAMB (*The Dowling House*): I find inspiration in news, photos, and songs.

CHARLES LYNNE (*What Screams In the Dark*): I usually get hit with an idea just by seeing something. Anything really, it doesn't matter. Then I try to find a way to turn it into something that would not be expected. I can be driving down the road and see a car stranded with no one in it, and I come up with how they got there, where they went, and what took them there. Also, possibly whether their bodies will ever be located.

MIKE PURFIELD (*In a Blackened Sky Where Dreams Collide*): Inspiration and ideas seem to come from three different areas. Primarily I consider my work bio-fiction. A large part of my emotional life and history is in the fiction. So if there is something I went through or going through or an event in the world that is affecting me, I will put it in the work.

The second area is meditation. I'm not big on mantra, point of focus, and closing my eyes. As an autistic, my brain works so hard I tend to fall asleep when I close my eyes for ten minutes. I found other ways to focus my mind, for example: reading and walking. When my mind is occupied with those activities, ideas or solutions or whatever pop into my head. Water does that too. Taking a shower has helped many of my books.

The third is more cognitive. I'm inspired by contrast. Most of my work is with series, so I have a set character(s) repeated over and over in different novels. In order to explore the character and to keep each book fresh and different from the first as best I can, I purposely throw them into situations or against characters that are different than before in hopes that it will show a different side. Sometimes the mundane situation can really bring out the most surprising reactions from your characters.

ISOBEL BLACKTHORN (*Clarissa's Warning*): Creating a new work is a strange process, and it's different each time. Sometimes, I feel a real buzz for a project, come up with a ton of ideas, create the setting, characters, plot, even write a few chapters and then, nothing. The muse just packs up and goes off somewhere else. The project loses its energy, and I shelve it, hoping one day in the future it will come alive again. I don't like waste.

As for my muse, she is Scarlet who must be obeyed. She wears a blood-red ball gown and runs barefoot through castles. She is wild, passionate, gothic, contrary, and wicked, and she likes to twist things. She gets very grumpy when I am not able to set her free. She sulks.

Once I have the basics of a story—a few characters, vague plot, and setting—then I wait. I wait and wait for hours and days for that first sentence to come through from her downstairs. I pace the floor. I need Scarlet to take control of the pen. Once she has it, things fly. But if we are interrupted by the ordinary stuff of life, she gets huffy and stomps off to her chamber, and to entice her back, I have to read through and edit whatever I have written so far. It can be a real chore, but she won't dive back in where we left off. I have to coax her back, tune in to the story, re-enter the flow. As you can imagine, I really detest those interruptions.

BOB VAN LAERHOVEN (*Return to Hiroshima*): When I'm feeling challenged during the writing process, I have a simple, 100-percent foolproof, but time- and energy-consuming trick up my sleeve. When I'm stuck or in doubt, I just write on and on. I imagine the weirdest bends and bridges in my story, and I write those mad episodes as if I was serious...until, suddenly, I'm on the right track again. You do not wait for inspiration. That would be a severe sin. You have to lure it: Muses want to be seduced by hard labor.

HEYWOOD GOULD (*Fort Apache, The Bronx*): Ideas just appear in my mind. I don't know why or how they got there. I assume they've been germinating in the muck of my subconscious until some external event or observation pushes them up to full and glorious fruition.

DAVID L. TAMARIN (*BOLO: Sociopaths on a Rampage*): I get all types of strange and bizarre ideas, and if I say something, people look at me funny, so I write it, and I don't know where that comes from. I do know a lot comes from research. I read a lot of nonfiction, especially true crime and psychology and sociology, and that helps with ideas as well as making stories more realistic. The main thing is strange personal experiences. My wife and I went to see my dentist once, and he works in a building with a lot of medical offices, one of which performed abortions. I was getting a cavity worked on, and there was this radical anti-abortion protest. They thought my wife and I were going for an abortion, and they surrounded us and attacked us. My first published story was "The Abortion People" in 2004, which was a horror story based on that incident.

BRET MCCORMICK (*Headhunters from Outer Space*): Have you ever gone shopping with a three-year-old child? It's a dazzling experience for the patient and perceptive adult. Every bright color, every odd shape, every mundane happenstance becomes fodder for the child's imagination. Questions and comments about absolutely everything pour out of the young mind almost faster than you can respond. And if you don't respond immediately, they are fiercely persistent! I've come to believe my muse is a three-year-old. Nothing in my life escapes her/his/its scrutiny. Consequently, there are more stories, essays, poems, and screenplay ideas piling up in my mental attic than I'll ever have the time in my remaining years to commit to words. Writer's block? What's that? Never experienced it. Doubt about the real value of what I've written? Sure, but I'm certain that's unavoidable. The things I actually sit down and write are the ones my muse screams loudest about. If an idea haunts me for months (or even years in some cases), I figure it is incumbent on me to turn it into something folks can read.

AUTUMN CHRISTIAN (*Girl Like a Bomb*): If I'm feeling stuck on a project, either in the beginning or end, first I gnash my teeth and wail on the floor like a giant baby. Okay, no, I don't really do that. Most of the time. It's still a frustrating experience and usually stems from the fact that I don't understand my characters or my aims as well as they do. So if I really can't go any further, I take a break—go for a walk or a shower, anything aimless. There's this idea of a default mode network in the human brain that is only activated when you're not concentrated on a task, and it relates to things like memory and creativity. I really do think the creative process is a lot of waiting around and giving your brain just enough information to do subconscious work. That being said, you have to make sure your brain is primed to do that. Ask questions, explore your characters, and seek out answers in your mind, even if nothing comes to you. Search out sensation, sound, and things that inspire you. A lot of creative work looks like sitting around, but it's far from just sitting around. (Although you'd be hard pressed to tell the difference looking at us, and we lie a lot about it.)

KURT BELCHER (*Spiders & Stardust*): For me, ideas come from anywhere. Music, books, movies, misheard phrases, random silly thoughts popping into my head… There really is no set inspiration. At the start, building an idea into a story worth reading is the exciting thing for me. Being asked to write a story around a certain character or even just a basic plot idea is a thrilling challenge, too. I particularly like turning something like that around quickly and to a degree of quality that I'm satisfied with. When I'm stuck, I generally try to get some thoughts moving on an unrelated idea. Sometimes, that helps me move past whatever's blocking me on the other idea. Other times, I bounce ideas off writer friends, try to find a work-around to the problem. But just as often, it's a matter of being alone, going for a walk, thinking about the problem while you're not staring at a computer screen. I don't write as much as I'd like, but who does, really?

KASEY PIERCE (*Pieces of Madness*): I'm a stickler for details in every conversation. Everything you say, the way you say it, and even your body language when you say it, is subject for inspiration. My friends, colleagues, and lovers are my captive lab mice.

Aside from that, memories from my upbringing and real-life events prompt a lot of inspiration. My mother's second battle with brain cancer became a catalyst for a fan favorite in my book *Pieces of Madness*, "His Majesty." When my sister-in-law asked how my mother was doing, an angry sob poured from me. "She can't just leave me here" was a response that even I was taken aback by…but I meant it. So the story begs the question "Are you more saddened by the loss of the person or a dissipating Utopia—the idea?" There's no wrong answer, really. But this gory tale pertains to the feeling of desperation and denial.

DEV JARRETT (*Loveless*): The ideas are everywhere, and when those ideas resonate and merge and create something new, or a new way to tell something old, it's an amazing feeling. Those ideas can sometimes feel like they're too big to handle, but it's all about finding the way in. One of the Army schools I attended was a cryptanalysis school, and beginning the solving of a cipher or a code works by a similar process. In a big, incomprehensible pile of code—or in the writer's case, a big pile of potential words that can be your start point—the cryppie (and the writer) will find that one detail that stands out. That detail in turn illuminates other details, and so on. The process continues until the cryptanalyst has the whole decrypted message, and the writer has the opening scene. From there, it's pretty much organic.

When I'm feeling challenged, whether it's a scene that I'm having trouble making work, or if I'm just feeling distracted, the best solution is usually just to put my head down over the keyboard and get the work done—words on paper, hitting the goal—even if it's crap. I keep going even if I can tell while I'm writing it that this line or that paragraph will get cut during editing. Get that first draft done, because you can't edit a blank page.

MELISSA KEIR (*Cowboy, Mine*): Small moments are my inspiration. Times I've lived, experiences, wishes, dreams, or "what if" moments. I use names of former students for the characters and have used snippets of words or conversations I've heard when I'm out in public. Yes, I do put what I hear into a story! But I also have been known to put people who I don't like into a story and send them through the wringer. So watch out!

I love small towns, having grown up in one and currently living in one. My stories are filled with children, pets and zaniness. Usually, it's the characters and what I believe will happen to them that gets me excited about writing their story. When I'm blocked, I go old school; I pull out a pad of paper and pen or pencil and start writing that way. Often, it's the self-editor in my head which holds me back. The idea is to get the words down and then edit later, but good intentions don't make for good roadways.

DAVID OWAIN HUGHES (*Brain Damage*): The thing that inspires me the most and fuels my dominatrix-like muse into action is the world around me: books, TV shows, films, newspapers/programs, comic books, graphic tales, snatches of overheard conversations, people-watching, long walks, periods of isolation, relaxation, tranquillity, bustle and noise, music, paintings, photos, and socializing. As a writer, you need to keep your eyes, ears, and mind open, because there are original stories to be told from all the activities going on around us on a constant basis. You just need to look.

Excitement for a project usually gets me going to begin with. Just like good foreplay, an idea will tease me into action, seducing the words from me until my muse is flowing (take that as you will!) and I'm at its full mercy. I mean, when a story proposal put forth by the creative brain is hot to trot, then it should spill out of an author in an insane fashion. Don't get me wrong, some ideas can be hard to write, whether it's because interest is lost or it's not your finest bit of writing, but you should always try and push through. I do, always, and you should *never* leave anything unfinished. That's an important rule to remember, because you'll never know when you might want/need that tale in the future.

JEFF PARSONS (*The Captivating Flames of Madness*): Ideas are all around you. Just pay attention. Objectively. If ideas don't come up to you drooling like clutching, needy children, try doing some new things in your life to get the creative spark glowing. Get out of your comfort zone. Collect some life experience. Have some (safe) adventures. Listen to people with different opinions than you. In my opinion, the best stories use real life experience with a 'what if' scenario thrown in.

I love thinking about plot twists. And I'm okay if an idea doesn't work out right away. Some never do. I have some bad ideas. Everyone does. Actually, I have many bad ideas. *Many. Bad. Ideas.* But like taking snapshots with a cell phone, you'll find a keeper here and there, so… take lots of pictures. And sometimes ideas just need to marinate for a while at a low simmer (preheat ancient red dragon to 450F for ten minutes). You can't force creativity. If it happens, sweet…roll with it! To encourage creativity, think about what's interesting and exciting to you and work off that. Seriously, what are you curious about?

When I feel overwhelmed, I give myself a time out and work on other aspects of writing (outlining, wordsmithing, editing, editing, editing, weeping bitter tears, staring into the abyss, wallowing in willful ignorance, etc.). I have several short story ideas going on at once, and lately, a novel to work on, so there are plenty of relevant distractions for me (along with coffee and chocolate and bright, shiny things). Keep some paper handy to write ideas down as you get them—just try to do it discreetly or else you'll scare the normal people. I also don't worry about writing. I do this for fun, so it should remain fun.

MICHAEL CIESLAK (*Desolation: 21 Tales for Tails*): Ideas come from everywhere. I can't remember who said it, but someone compared the collection of ideas to composting. You take one idea here, another there, let them stew together for a while, and you end up with something fertile which will support your story. I also read a lot. I read plenty of genre fiction, but also a lot of nonfiction. The most amazing story ideas can come from histories, biographies, and the like.

The beginning of a project is the easy part. That's when you are super excited, and everything seems bright and your idea is the most brilliant thing that has ever been written. The difficult part is when the doubts start to creep in. I'll be honest, when it starts to get tough, I cheat. I usually have three or four things that I am working on at any given time. When one starts to bog down, I switch over to another. I hopscotch between projects until everything is finished.

Speaking of finished, another great motivator is a deadline. Whether it is a hard deadline set by a publisher or a self-imposed one, there is nothing like the circled date on a calendar to make me push on.

PHIL PRICE (*Unknown*): Life inspires me. I take lots of my inspiration from news stories, both old and new. I normally have a ton of ideas before I start, plotting how the book will play out. But sometimes, you just have to go with the flow. When writer's block rears its ugly head, I normally stop writing for a week or so, trying to imagine how it should play out in my head. Which is interesting, as my head is normally filled-to-capacity. I need a clear-out!

JESSE DEDMAN (*The Master's Torment*): Inspiration just creeps up on me. I could be driving to work, and an idea just pops in. After a while of entertaining the thoughts, I'll get the urge to put it down somehow. The muse is not all that different from sex. When the mood strikes, it strikes. You can ignore it and be frustrated with yourself, or you can act upon it and feel much, much better.

JAMES WATTS (*Them*): I'm not really sure I have a muse. I will say that I have been inspired by '80s horror. When I start a story, it forms from some random idea and speaks to me. I follow the story as it unfolds and always stay true to it.

A.P. SESSLER (*The First Suitor*): I'm a serial pacer. If I have enough room to make a circle, my brain will kick into gear, and the ideas will roll. There's one trail I walk to take in nature—it's so good for the body, the soul, and the creative process. It's also a good way to move that pesky writer's block out of your way. My other source of inspiration are my crazy, lucid dreams.

Concerning motivation, I have plenty, but I always have a dozen projects going at once, whether it's artistic, musical, or literary. I go where inspiration leads. If I'm not feeling it on one project, I visit another. It's a slow process, and I wish I could start something and stick with it until the end, but it's not how my brain works.

JASON PARENT (*A Life Removed*): Ideas can come from anywhere. Dreams, everyday life, even calls for submissions—all have inspired me to place words on a page. And once that inspiration hits, I want to run with it and complete the work while the passion is still hot. Once that love for the idea fades, I need to put it aside until I rethink it and fall in love with it all over again.

STANLEY B. WEBB (short story writer, numerous anthologies): I'm not sure where my ideas come from. They tend to appear in my mind, and I jot them down. Usually, nothing develops from an idea, but sometimes, one lingers and grows in my imagination. A story might linger for months before I start to write.

WADE H. GARRETT (*Pigs: An Extreme Horror Novella*): Vigilantism is my primary area of writing. I get my ideas from what I'd do to someone if I was wanting vengeance. Combine that with a dark mind, and the ideas come flowing out.

RICHARD CHRISTIAN MATHESON (*Scars and Other Distinguishing Marks*): Aberration. Its roots and details lead to stories. Human psychology is the starting point for everything I write. My plots are usually explored symptoms.

ANDREW LENNON (*Bound*): The first muse is most certainly my wife! Forget writing, I didn't even like reading until my mid-twenties, and it was my wife who pushed me to try King, and then other books. Eventually, I stumbled across Goodreads. After rating books I liked, I was suggested The Summer I Died by Ryan C. Thomas in books I may like to read. Wow. I read that book, and it completely blew me away! I wanted to make something like that. So, I casually mentioned to my wife that I was going to have an attempt at writing my own book. She was massively supportive and pushed me to keep going even when I felt like I wanted to give up on it.

Years later, I have now worked with Ryan on several projects and his publishing company, Grand Mal Press, has actually re-branded and republished my debut novel. It was a bit of a dream come true.

Now when I'm trying to get myself in the mood to write, I usually read a few short stories. I'll put on the horror channel or some old cheesy horror film, and then I'll lock myself away in my bedroom and just write. I can usually tell if it's going to be a good story or not by how much fun I have while writing it.

PEGGY CHRISTIE (*Hell Hath No Fury*): Most anything in every day life can be inspiring for a story. One of the more random ones was overhearing a young boy talking to his grandma at the diner. He asked aloud, "Remember this morning when dad was torturing me?" I immediately put down my forkful of pork sausage and blueberry pancake and wrote that down. It ended up becoming a short story about a family that tortures people, something they do together that's been a tradition for generations. I always keep some sort of notebook in my purse for just such occasions. Inspiration can happen anytime, anywhere.

The main thing that gets me going on a project is simply being excited about creating it, especially in the beginning;. Something fresh and completely different from anything else I've done at that point. A buddy of mine and I are working on this really cool idea, and the first installment is done. I have a notebook filled with scribbles of other ideas in the same series. Now, when the shine wears off, I do become a bit more stubborn (read: lazy) about doing the work, or I simply can't see the story's progression. That's when booze helps. Maybe coffee. Sometimes together—like a reward system. Most times, when I get stuck, I turn to another project to try and shake things up.

CHRISTOPH PAUL (*A Confederacy of Hot Dogs*): Wanting to empathize, understand, or experience something I can't in my limited reality. Sometimes it can be a friend, an article, or just a thought that comes to me when I'm doing something random like working out or doing landscaping, and I want to explore it more. I write songs, and it is a similar process in that I get obsessed with an idea, character, or story.

BILLY CHIZMAR (*Widow's Point*): I've identified two kinds of creative ideas that I have. The first kind of ideas are the plot or setting-driven ones, the "what ifs…" and the kinds of things that are genuinely fun to dream up and wonder about. These are the ideas separate from myself, ideas that anyone could have, and they're fun because they don't hurt. They don't hurt because nothing's at stake. The second kind is a bitch. This kind comes from the same place my eyes sink into when I feel like I could cry. When these ideas occur to me, they sink into my forehead until I write them down on paper and offload their weight. They are the evolution of the first kind of idea. They are what happens when the "what if a college was infested with vampires and no one can tell who?" becomes "what if my college was infested with vampires and I can't tell if the guy I've lived with for four years, the guy who got me through my breakup with Daisy, the guy who I spent eight hours in the library studying for a class we'd attended a combined total of seven times, was going to puncture my neck with his own two front fangs in my sleep?" If I can't put myself into an idea then it's worthless. There's a lot of really fun stuff sitting in my notebook because they haven't made that evolutionary leap into emotion yet.

JOE X. YOUNG (short-story writer, numerous anthologies): My muse has always been straightforward in that I write for a variety of reasons, many of which are "just because," by which I mean "just because I happen to be in the right place at the right time to see/hear/feel something which inspires me to write." I'm lucky in that my fiancée Annett is a gift to me as well as gifted in her own right, and she will regularly have an idea of something I should write, and then she'll help me develop it. I'm fortunate in that even without Annett's input, I am never starved for an idea.

A story may be prompted by a call out for an anthology, or just for fun, however, I read a lot, watch films and TV, and will sometimes be left disappointed and thinking "that would have been better if…" So, instead of bitching about it, I go off and write my take on the subject.

When I'm feeling challenged? Well, I have a lot of challenges anyway as I have many physical disabilities and Asperger's syndrome, so I'm no stranger to things being difficult. I was "high-functioning autistic" before it became fashionable and didn't get therapy/treatment or even understanding. I never feel as if writing a story is a challenge in itself, as I've had far worse to contend with, but meeting deadlines, word counts, and generally attempting to shoehorn the subject matter to suit the prompt can be restrictive as I much prefer to just "go with the flow." All challenges are set to be overcome, and if I can't rise above these things, then I don't deserve to be taken seriously as a writer.

DEAN M. DRINKEL (*Demonologica Biblica*): When I first started out [my muse] was mainly alcohol! Now, that is not something I am recommending at all, but for me, there is definitely a correlation between the booze and writing—both of which I started when I was at university. Whenever we students used to go out to the pubs and clubs, I always made sure that I had a notepad with me, because as soon as I began imbibing, words and sentences began to form in my brain, and I'd start noting them down. This was a great boon for me as a writer, but it also led to a few nasty moments as sometimes other drinkers and customers thought I was writing about them! I'd get called out for fights or get called names, but hey ho, I had the last laugh, didn't I?

Nowadays, the drink is less important to me (though I still love a pint or glass of wine when I can), and I suppose I can find inspiration literally anywhere. I might hear a phrase in a song or a poem, and I'll store it away in the old noggin for a time when it can become usable. I have books and books filled to the brim (that's one of those mixed metaphor things, isn't it?) with words, phrases, and titles which I will reread from time to time to get the brain muscle flexing. Religion is also a great muse for me, and even recently, a friend who is writing a story for one of my future anthos had been trailing through the New Testament and found something of real interest. All it takes is a word or two, and (if you know your stuff, obviously) you can create something special. Places are also important to me, and even as I type this, I am thinking of Paris and can actually smell it in my nostrils—so that will inspire me to no end. People, too—if I start thinking of someone (it doesn't matter if I like them or not) and my pen is poised, well, the world can be my oyster for sure.

EVANS LIGHT (*Black Door*): Inspiration often arises at the most unlikely times and from the most unexpected sources. Some may strike you as brilliant, others as obvious and mundane, but I try my best not to let any potential story idea pass by without capturing it for later. An idea is like a passing mist that quickly disperses if not crystallized and preserved in some way the moment it arrives.

Though some authors may argue this point, story ideas aren't freshly-baked bread. Unless an idea is extremely topical, a genuinely solid plot or concept can stay fresh for a while. The same can't always be said for your enthusiasm, though. Clearly it's a balance. If you have ideas arriving frequently you can't expect to properly execute them all simultaneously, especially if you ever want to have projects reach completion.

Don't be afraid to store them for later, as some ideas will become better as time is spent, both consciously and unconsciously, reflecting upon them. I'm often surprised at how much work the subconscious mind can accomplish. Upon occasion, story ideas that were previously mere fragments bubble up to the surface fully formed, my conscious mind caught completely unaware that I'd been working the story out deep inside all along.

JAMES H. LONGMORE (*Pede*): For me, ideas come from pretty much anywhere and everywhere—but they do delight in tormenting me by popping up in those dark, shadowy moments around the Devil's hour, mid-shower, or in the middle of a Pixar movie when it is impossible to write them down. Oftentimes, they stick around, but every now and then, one will slip away and skulk at the periphery of my memory from where it may best taunt me.

The thrill of the new is often more than enough to have me clamoring for the keyboard, that heady excitement of meeting brand-new characters and unfolding tales of terror—the hard part comes halfway through, when the creative brain is itching to move on to the next project and the one that was once so fresh and exhilarating feels like an aging family member who really ought to be confined to a rest home.

MEGAN O'RUSSELL (*Girl of Glass*): I've found inspiration in many different ways. The concept for my mid-apocalyptic sci-fi series, complete with chemically-induced vampires, came from a bet with my husband. He didn't think blending sci-fi, dystopian, and fantasy could work in a cohesive form. I wrote *Girl of Glass* to prove him wrong.

Another story came out of a freezing cold hike where my husband was bemoaning the fact that there isn't an app on a phone to start you an emergency fire. Us coming up with a list of what magical apps you'd want on a phone became *The Tale of Bryant Adams*.

A lot of locations have also created worlds I wasn't even looking to build. From a maze lake in Thailand to greenhouses and botanical gardens all over the United States, there are some things I see and know I want to write the details of a place—the smell, the way the sunrise looks—into a book.

When I'm feeling completely stuck on a project, the best solution I've found is to go hiking. There comes a point when your legs are so tired and your brain is so numb from just trying to put one foot in front of the other, creating imaginary worlds where you aren't still climbing uphill becomes a wonderful release. Your brain can't continue its self-inflicted writer's block when it has conquering mountains to worry about.

ANDREW BUCKLEY (*Hair in All the Wrong Places*): I speak a lot in schools about where to find inspiration, and I wish I could point to one single thing, but it really comes down to imagination and stories that resonate with you. I've found if the idea doesn't resonate with you on some level, then it'll end up getting abandoned (and I have a folder full of partial manuscripts to prove it). My motivation is usually fueled by my publisher and/or agent and the requirement to meet a deadline. On a side note, deadlines are horrible things and should be wiped from the face of the earth.

JOHN BODEN (*Jedi Summer with the Magnetic Kid*): I wish I had a great answer for this. Out of the blue is the honest answer as to where I get ideas. Sometimes slivers from dreams or just every day occurrences that upon reflection can be warped in a way.

LAURA ROBERTS (*Haiku for Lovers*): My day job involves transcription for reality TV, so I get a lot of inspiration from the things these ordinary folks are talking about. Most of the shows are unscripted, so I'm writing down a back-and-forth conversation between a character and the producer as they work out a storyline together. Although people often denigrate reality TV as being sensational or fake, I think they also forget these shows are about real people, with real problems (with the possible exception of the Real Housewives...), and they're all doing the best they can. I find them all fascinating personalities with unique voices, and just listening to those conversations on a daily basis helps keep my ear for dialogue sharp.

ERIN SWEET AL-MEHAIRI (*Breathe, Breathe*): I often take walks, go to galleries or other museums, to libraries, or most of all, massive bodies of water like Lake Erie. I find my muse in things I see in nature, in paintings, in reading about myths and legends or history, in staring at the water or up at the skies. I find it also in everyday horrors and traumas I've been through or I see others go through. I find inspiration in so many things all around me every day, even cookies.

H.R. BOLDWOOD (*The Corpse Whisperer*): On occasion, I listen to Vampyre Syndicate, chamber music, or other melodies without words. Sometimes, reading before I write gets my mind moving in the right direction. My ideas often come from watching science programs and asking, what if? Combining science and history with my over-the-top imagination and sense of humor produces the most creative results.

JULIA BRAMER (*The Vitamin D Treatment*): My muse usually visits when I am not trying. Most especially in my sleep and in that in-between time between sleep and being awake. I keep a notepad by my bed to catch the lines and ideas she delivers to me. The other time she seems to strike is while exercising. Recording then is not nearly as convenient, but in a pinch, my smart phone can become a voice recorder during a jog or a memo pad during weight lifting. There is also something to be said for the powers of memory and recitation until you get home to get it down.

RANDEE DAWN (*Home for the Holidays*): I keep the muse in a small box in the drawer of my desk and occasionally provide her with tears of children who happen to wander by. Okay, truth: I don't really think of "conjuring" a muse, per se. I think of writing as a continuum of information/experiences in, stories out. It's like a very long inhale/exhale: There needs to be time when you're breathing in the world, living your life and masticating it—and then you switch to repurposing it into stories and tales that interweave disparate concepts and experiences and considerations and characters. The muse is always with us, but she must be fed, and sometimes she needs to rest. Understanding this as a process means I tend not to panic about writer's block. As for ideas—anything is fertile territory. As my husband likes to say, "No one is safe around a writer." I've been inspired by personal experience—and by funny street sign names. Everything is fodder.

LANNY LARCINESE (*I Detest All My Sins*): My whole damned life has been a writing prompt. It helps to have been a risk-taker, lived in different towns, done a variety of things to make money, come from a semi-wacko family, been married twice, been on the couch, lived inside cities, been philosophic and a compulsive communicator. I don't conjure the muse—she pesters me.

KATE JONEZ (*Lady Bits*): Ideas for stories are everywhere. That's the easy part. I started having success when I applied the tools of method acting to writing. I like to inhabit the character's life. I get to a higher level of insight when I walk through the world and say and do things the character would.

SCOTT M. GORISCAK (*Horrorism*): Many of my ideas come from my everyday observations, experiences, and dreams. I travel extensively with my real-time position, sometimes to very unusual places around the United States. This affords me many opportunities to observe different regions, people, and places not usually on the beaten path. I document my thoughts in a travel journal that I keep with me, then transcribe into my WIP folders. When I have extensive windshield time, I dictate my thoughts and story ideas into my cell phone. Lastly, I keep a dream journal next to my bed at night. I do this so I don't miss a creative opportunity. You never know when a great idea will present itself.

ADRIENNE DELWO (*Hero Academy*): I get inspiration from everywhere—personal experiences, history, news stories, role-playing games, random photographs... I most often respond to the idea of who a character is, and then my brain begins to construct stories around them.

ESSELL PRATT (*Sharkantula*): I find that my muse lingers within my imagination. Whether a blessing or a curse, I am not certain. I find that ideas are born from random happenings around me, whether it be a leaf falling in front of me, a song on the radio, or a movement out of the corner of my eye, my muse provides the inspiration to turn that insignificant moment into something much more than what it actually was.

GEORGE LEA (*Strange Playgrounds*): Ever since I was a child, I have experienced imaginative play that was removed from what peers, siblings, and friends expressed; states, creatures, and worlds so vivid I could physically see and hear and feel them. This often distressed those around me, as I would lose myself in those worlds to the point whereby waking reality became something quite different. In the years since, that hasn't waned, but I have learned to direct it, to express it on the page. This is essential to my psychological well-being; if I was prevented from doing so, I would fear for my sanity. As a result, what I produce is often hallucinatory, expressing the fluidity of reality itself. In that, the inner workings of my mind, my neuroses become the stuff of storytelling; demons that are desperate to express themselves but which I am not at all eager to exorcise.

ERIC J. GUIGNARD (*That Which Grows Wild*): For me, ideas come, literally and figuratively, from everywhere: Dreams (both night and day), global news and current affairs, conversations with people, personal observations of the world, and playing the "What If?" game.

MERCEDES M. YARDLEY (*Pretty Little Dead Girls*): I wish I could conjure my muse with candles and a soft voice, and sometimes I can. I see her very clearly. I wrote about her in a story called "Show Your Bones." She's gaunt and ethereal and full of suffering, but she's so wise and eloquent. I live in a tiny, chaotic home full of children, pets, and disorder, and it's difficult for me to write in such a state. I need to quiet things down so I can hear the padding footsteps and the whispers of my muse. I soften the lights. I put in headphones. I turn my back to the pandemonium and that's when I can concentrate. It's usually in short spurts, about fifteen minutes at a time, but it's how I'm forced to work. And she comes, this muse. She whispers. She doesn't shout. Sometimes there's an urgency to her whispering, but it's always quiet. It's like when people talk about hearing the promptings of God. If I'm not listening, I don't catch it. My muse refuses to shout.

ROBERT FORD (*The God Beneath My Garden*): When I was young, I learned quickly that I was allowed to stay up late at family gatherings if I stayed quiet and observed. That lesson stuck with me, and I get ideas by observing people and my surroundings combined with asking "what if?" I also almost always get my titles first, even though I may not have the story attached to it. Having a great title automatically kicks in my muse to figure out what the title means. I also pay attention to weird news articles, and very often, that will spark some story concept with a twist. I've also never been afraid to mine my own (sometimes painful) experiences and put a metaphorical spin on it. Some of my most (emotionally) bloody stories have come from doing that.

HOPE CLARK (*Murder on Edisto*): I've always disliked the word "muse," like it's apart and separate from my intellect and creative mind. Like she's out of my control. I fully believe that we are in complete control of our creativity. Not that it's spontaneous, and it might take months, even years, to come around and gel, but it is still all me, all us. But where do my ideas come from? Mine start with place. My soul is deeply entrenched in nature, so when I started my first series, I steeped it in rural South Carolina, a setting I know and love. Envisioning myself in place allows me to become the character and experience the crime (I write traditional mystery). When I was asked by my publisher to diversify and start a second series, she knew enough about me to tell me to select one remarkable place to set it and then take it from there. I chose Edisto Beach, South Carolina. Once I determine place, I settle into it, research it, visit it, feel it, and from there, I become the story. But I don't have a muse. When under contract for a book, I simply sit and write. My muse can show up or be gone. I don't care. I'm writing the damn story whether she's there or not.

W.B.J. WILLIAMS (*The Garden at the Roof of the World*): I find my muse in listening to music and looking at art in museums. Ideas will also spring to mind in meditation.

MARTIN ROSE (*Bring Me Flesh, I'll Bring Hell*): I think it's about time we de-mythologize the muse. This isn't a mystical process. This can be learned. The ideas come from within, they always have. When I was very young, ideas came to me, because everything is fresh and new and dynamic and I was inexperienced. You think your ideas are original, but you discover that's not the case. Your ideas have already been thought of. So where does that leave you? If you want to build a better pathway to controlling the quality of your ideas, and always being able to tap into new ideas at any given moment, you have to always be learning, always be listening, always be observing, always be exposing yourself to ideas. The more unconnected and diverse, the better, and it helps to recognize patterns. The things you learn and pay attention to become the prima materia—the first materials, as they say in alchemy. Next, add pressure. Add a deadline. Add friction to your way of thinking. Some of the greatest ideas are inventions brought about by the need to problem solve. If you're really stuck, find a problem. Solve it with your story.

PEGGY A. WHEELER (*Chaco*): My ideas come from everywhere and everything. Examples: The original idea for my allegorical fantasy, *The Splendid and Extraordinary Life of Beautimum Potamus*, came from re-watching Disney's *Fantasia*. The storyline for my supernatural mystery-thriller, *The Raven's Daughter*, came after I had attended several Bear Dances hosted by a Modoc medicine man in northern California. I was deeply moved and knew I had to write a story including the Bear Dance and indigenous lore and mythology. The idea for my dystopian-adventure, *Chaco*, came from an article on sun storms I read in *National Geographic*. The article inspired me to research Coronal Mass Ejections (CME) and to write a story about "what if" a series of powerful Class X CMEs directly hit Earth today. I get ideas while listening to music, watching the news, listening to other people's conversations, in the shower, while driving—especially if I happen to see pair of coyotes, each with a rabbit in its mouth, which did happen. Anything that piques the imagination serves as my muse. I don't conjure my muse, I simply pay attention to the world around me; she's everywhere.

TODD KEISLING (*The Smile Factory*): I usually conjure my muse with a few candles, some esoteric symbols drawn on the floor, and incantations from an unholy book bound in human flesh. And by all that, I really mean the ideas come from anything and everything, from random what-if scenarios that pop into my head to my daydreams and nightmares.

LORI R. LOPEZ (*The Strange Tale of Oddzilla*): I basically wait for ideas to find me. And they do. Sometimes they chase me. They also have a habit of arriving at the worst moments, when I cannot scribble them down. I am prone to forgetting all but the most vivid notions if not recorded promptly. Some ideas are like ghosts, attempting to contact me from The Beyond after slipping away. I've been meaning to get a Crystal Ball and see if that might provide a link. I've lost too many... Others clamor for attention. They are not very good about forming a line and waiting their turn. Seriously. I'm being serious. They have a habit of popping into my head out of nowhere. And if I should try to think of an idea, I may be avalanched, bombarded, deluged. The ones I manage to get down before they're gone can sit around for years. And years. Then, suddenly, it's the right time! It starts spreading, blossoming...like a vine. Or a weed. Before long it's a jungle with tentacles writhing out my ears.

PAUL FLEWITT (*Poor Jeffrey*): I once read an interview with Ramsey Campell where he spoke about ideas, and he spoke about getting his ideas from Muse Monthly, and they sent you an idea a month with your subscription. Just a jest, but I really wish that was a thing sometimes. Seriously though, ideas can come from anywhere: an interesting landmark or structure, the daily news, odd comments spoken in the middle of a conversation, a curious person you might see on the street. With me, names conjure up story ideas a lot. I think of a name, or see a name somewhere and I start writing that person's story in my head. Other times, it's an opening line that comes first and the story springs off from there.

GIL VALLE (*A Gathering of Evil*): I never imagined that I would become an author with three books published, and more on the way. I was a B+ level writer in AP Literature in high school, and I would have called you crazy if you told me that fifteen years later I would be writing novels and that I would have a pretty decent number of fans, considering the genre that I write.

But necessity is the mother of invention. After being the center of the very public and incredibly embarrassing "Cannibal Cop" case, I felt compelled to tell my full story in a memoir. Writing Raw Deal was difficult because I forced myself to relive everything about how my life was destroyed, but it was also cathartic. Most importantly, I really enjoyed the entire process of getting a book published, and around the time Raw Deal came out, many people suggested that I should try writing horror novels. I guess it made sense, since my horror writing in Internet chat rooms was so realistic that it got me in trouble with the FBI.

So, I can't definitively say that anything tangible helps me find ideas. I just realized that I enjoyed writing and I went for it, and with the "Cannibal Cop" stigma forever attached to me, extreme horror was the way to go. When *A Gathering of Evil* came out, it received a lot of publicity because of my background and that really helped get the word out. I didn't know what to expect after that.

JESSICA MCHUGH (*Rabbits in the Garden*): Everything and nothing inspires me. From the most dazzling objects and situations to the most mundane, I'm always searching for the next story hiding in plain sight. And because I live off of story sales, I never wait for an idea to strike. If I don't seek them out, I can't afford my lovely writing sessions at local bars, and that just won't do.

SCOTT M. BAKER (*Nazi Ghouls from Space*): My muse appears in unexpected places—news stories, artwork, conversations with my wife. The whole concept of Hell Gate originated while watching an early episode of SyFy Channel's Face Off in which one of the make-up artists depicted Red Riding Hood as a bad-ass werewolf killer with a mini-gun for a right hand. That eventually morphed into Sasha, one of the book's main characters and around whom the plot is based. I'm fortunate that my muse is so creative but, on the downside, I have more plot ideas than I have time to write.

J. STEFFY (*Evolution of a Monster*): My dreams inspire me. I tend to remember most of my dreams. I quickly write down any good ideas I had before they vanish. To get going, I just start writing about what I'm drawn to. If I lose interest while writing, I'll retire the story and start another. Maybe I'll go back one day and maybe not.

S.A. COSBY (*My Darkest Prayer*): I love perusing books of black and white photography. Or going to an art gallery. Visual stimulation awakens my creativity. I'll see a painting or a photo and begin to tell myself a story about it. If I like the story I write it down.

J.C. MICHAEL (*Pandemonium*): I wouldn't say I live an exciting life, but the day to day is what inspires me, and all I need to do is expand upon that and take it somewhere that does provide some excitement, interest, or in the case of most of my writing, horror. Write what you know may be a cliche, but if you ground your work in something you know about then your work will hopefully come across as something genuine, and maybe even relatable. As for when the muse strikes for me to twist the facts of everyday experience and evolve them into something that works as a piece of fiction, well, that seems to happen when it happens. It can't be forced, although a rapidly approaching deadline can act as an incentive!

CHAD LUTZKE (*The Same Deep Water as You*): While uninvited ideas pop up all the time, I do my best to keep them at bay until I'm ready. Otherwise, I find myself writing three books at a time. When I *am* ready, it doesn't take much more than sitting quietly, staring out a window or gazing at the floor and some kind of birthing transpires and I'll write it down. I find inspiration in memories, photographs, music, and hypothetical "What If's". I'm a curious and observant person who asks a lot of questions, so it's fun to create situations by mixing in aspects of my own life. It's a blessing, really.

EDWARD LEE (*White Trash Gothic*): You know, it really is an automatic thing, I think. Everybody's born with an aptitude for something; writers are born with an aspect of creativity. The ideas are always cooking in a certain kind of mind, so there's no real concrete impetus. Sometimes, a simple errant image will cause a creative brainstorm, sometimes a newspaper article, sometimes something you overhear a stranger say. I never stop thinking of stories and scenarios—it's in my psyche. What a wonderful curse!

RHONDA PARRISH (*Fae*): Anything. Everything. Usually I get stories in fragments. I overhear someone on the bus say something slightly unusual—fragment. I'm watching a television documentary about migrant workers who trim marijuana—fragment. I hear an interesting phrase that sounds like it could be a title on the radio—fragment. All those fragments get tossed into the slow cooker that is my subconscious and left there until a few of them stick together and float to the surface as a story seed.

RICHARD GODWIN (*Savage Highway*): Life itself inspires me. There are so many occasions, so many everyday incidents, one can draw inspiration from. Often then, I am left asking myself the question of whether readers would believe what I just saw.

BARBARA ELLE (*Death in Vermillion*): I find inspiration every day, in everyday life. *Death In Vermillion* was inspired by conversations with a good friend who is an artist, who told me funny stories about her art studio and fellow artists. Then I thought, what if one of them was found murdered? My characters are often inspired by people I know, sort of like casting a movie, which helps me create three-dimensional characters who are distinct from each other—and often in conflict. Character and conflict inspire each scene and create an arc for the narrative.

STEPHEN SPIGNESI (*Dialogues*): I have more ideas than I'll likely ever be able to bring to fruition. I have six unpublished novels written, plus the starts of many more. My agent has more than fifty nonfiction book proposals that he sends out on a regular basis. I've written full-time for around thirty years, and one thing I've learned is that you cannot wait for inspiration. Oh, it's terrific when it comes, and I'll gladly exploit it, but a writer needs to develop the thought processes that looks at everything and asks "Is this a book?"

Sometimes I get stalled. But I resist the temptation to refer to this as "writer's block." Richard Christian Matheson and I talked about this, and he said he doesn't think writer's block is an actual "block." He thinks it's a change of mood, and he gets out of it by doing something else and then coming back to whatever he was stuck on.

GREG HICKEY (*The Friar's Lantern*): In terms of starting a new project, I'm inspired by my interactions with ideas, which usually come by way of reading. Whether novels or the newspaper, most of my work begins when I encounter an idea that calls me to respond in some way. Maybe it's a plot line in a novel that I think should develop differently. Maybe it's a research paper about a new idea or an emerging technology. Maybe it's an issue in the news that keeps coming up again and again without a satisfactory solution. I try to write down any ideas that seem interesting. If I can't get one out of my head after a few days, I know I have the basis for a story.

In terms of writing a new section within a project, I find that physical movement usually stimulates my creativity. There's scientific evidence that walking helps the creative process, and I've definitely found that to be true. When I'm feeling at a loss for words, I'll take a notebook or my phone and go for a walk outside. I've composed entire chapters and essays while walking around and stopping to write two or three sentences at a time.

M. NAIDOO (*Where Sleeping Lies Lie*): I wish there was a surefire way to turn on those creative juices. For me, inspiration can strike any time and often in the most unexpected places. My brain seems to be stuck in discovery mode that never sleeps. I'll wake up at two in the morning with an idea that just won't let me go back to sleep. I can be on the treadmill listening to my work-out jam, out walking the dog, doing dishes, or watching a movie when the solution to a plot problem hits. There is no pattern, which is somewhat annoying since I can't control it. On the upside, I can count on it to hit sooner or later. That's just the way it is for me.

BEN OHMART (*The Rerun of Dracula*): My superego or id develops my ideas. I wake up or am in the shower and they pop up. Sometimes I'll think of something based on another idea since I like comedy writing mostly, but most of the time a new idea just appears like a billboard sign. Whether I jot it down or act on it later is another matter.

B.R. STATEHAM (*Murder Is Our Business*): I don't find my muse, she finds me. All the time. Stories pop into my head, many times unwanted. By 'stories,' I actually mean images. Images pop into my head that set up the entire novel. From that first image, I create the whole novel. One image at a time. Think of it as movie clips written as prose. I string a whole series of movie clips together, hoping that in the process, it comes out coherent for the reader.

DOUGLAS BRODE (*Sweet Prince: The Passion of Hamlet*): Please note that I am an 'anti-muse' writer. In fact, I believe the reason that I produced so little writing—good, bad, or indifferent—when I was young (college age and right after) is that I was listening for the muse, and she was strangely silent. I would sit down to write and, not feeling particularly inspired, end up going to a movie, thinking: the time was not ripe... if I try writing something important now, it will likely be not as good as it would have been had I held on until a magic light descended like the one that covers Pinocchio as he comes to life. What horse shit! The best thing that ever happened to me was getting a job as a journalist. Because then you have to produce or you are out. I did a column three days a week, and there was no time to wait and hope for a moment of genius. I turned out whatever I could, always the best that I could at that moment. When I finally left that occupation and switched back to my first love—writing fiction—I held on to the same approach.

What did someone say? "A writer writes..." Do not talk about what you are going to write with friends, family, or fellow writers, for then the story goes out of you, and writing it down doesn't seem so important as you have 'shared' it on some level. Set a particular time to work, and do not vary from it. Write for between one and two hours every day. Don't stop to worry if it is any good or not. That comes later. Just keep turning out the words. Most of them will be not as great as you hoped and dreamed, but far better than you feared during your darkest moments. As to ideas and where they come from…what interests you most? Decide, and write about that. I used to try writing in what I thought were salable genres at any one period in time. Like hippie-era fiction in the mid-1960s. Then I realized: what I love most is history. So my first published novel, Sweet Prince, was based on the actual (not Shakespeare's version) Hamlet/Amuleth of Denmark. I'm currently consumed with a three-book retelling of the life of Jesus as it has never been presented before, trying to figure out what might have been the very explicable reality behind supposed "miracles." I'm always reading books on history for pleasure. Now I write novels inspired by them. It's my way. Go find your own.

The Writing Process

STEWART O'NAN (*Snow Angels*): I just go day to day, picking up where I left off, hoping I'll eventually make it to the end and that I'll find surprises on the way. When I do, I'm relieved and happy. And then I have to start again.

MICHELLE BOWSER (*A Gross Miscellany*): When I begin a writing project, I work on it every day as much as I can and take long breaks between projects. The environment is whatever I'm stuck in at the time. Usually my home office, but if I have to be in other places, I take along my tablet and get to work wherever I can.

ANDY RAUSCH (*Bloody Sheets*): I try to make myself write, even when I don't want to. Unless I'm exhausted to the point where I am certain that I will only muck up the piece, I write. If I just feel uninspired, I still make myself write. I remember Neil Gaiman saying something that has always stuck with me. He said something to the effect of, "I wrote every day, even on the days when I didn't feel like writing. And in the end, when I went back and looked at the finished draft, I honestly couldn't tell the difference between the inspired days and the uninspired days." But beyond that, it doesn't even really matter, because that's what rewrites are for. The first draft is sort of there to just get the ideas down on paper. Rewrites are where you really mold the piece and figure out what works and what doesn't.

MARK SLADE (*A Six Gun & the Queen of Light*): I've written in loud and chaotic environments. Lately it's been 10 a.m., a cup of coffee in hand, and headphones piping music into my ears. I usually just write enough so I that I have just enough left for the next day to write.

GARY VINCENT (*Darkened Hills*): I write a great deal, although in all honesty, I can't really quantify the amount. I don't sit down each day and say, "Well, I need to make a 1,500 word limit before I stop." In my day-to-day job, I do a lot of technical writing. I also head a writers' cooperative and find myself doing some proofing as well, which sometimes impacts my personal goals for any given day.

My best writing environment is someplace quiet and isolated. In today's busy world, this has been my biggest challenge. My attention tends to drift too much to what's going on, and that affects the quality of writing. If I can break away to someplace remote, then the better stuff emerges.

BECKY NARRON (short-story writer, numerous anthologies): I'm lucky because I have a talent to tune everything around me out. So that lets me write anywhere. When the mood strikes me, I write. Sometimes it's days before I write again, but when I do, it's a lot. I just hold the pen. I tend to know either the beginning or the end to them and then fill in the blanks. I can't use a timeline—it just doesn't work for me. Besides, they tend to go where they want to anyway. Stubborn little buggers.

JOE R. LANSDALE (*Bubba Ho-Tep*): I prefer to write at home in my office, but I can write almost anywhere if needed, and as I travel a lot these days, I've learned to write in hotels, sometimes on the plane, on a train. That's not my preferred method, but I can do it. I carry my laptop with me most of the time so I can do that. I like to get up in the morning and work about three hours, and then that's it. I try to leave my work where I feel I could go just a bit further, and then I try not to think about it until the next morning, otherwise it can have a run-over-by-a-truck feeling. Like you've investigated the idea too much. I like to feel fresh. I work just about every day. Since I work three hours or so, though now and again I'll do an afternoon or late night session, I always feel like I'm having fun and I'm excited about the next day, and I can maintain this pace mostly seven days a week. I'll take time off now and again, but I know the difference between taking time off and goofing off. This way, even on my birthday and holidays, I can work and not feel I've robbed myself of time. I also managed most weeks to read about three books, and I watch film and TV, and try to read newspapers and a variety of things. Ideas can come from anywhere and anything. I keep a lot of stuff in front of me. I also teach and practice martial arts and visit with people and travel. Those provide ideas as well, and it keeps your work more real, without the constant stink of the library on it, which is no criticism of libraries. But I like to, unlike Lovecraft, write things that sound like what people would say, people with jobs, and sometimes families, and real lives.

CHRIS ROY (*Her Name Is Mercie*): [Note: Chris, an accomplished author, is serving a life sentence in prison.] I scribble notes on scraps of whatever is near at the time, and then later write first drafts by hand. I'll write a page or three, then type it up in Google Docs on my phone. I've never used a computer or word processor. For some reason, the prison administration is adverse to providing us with Internet access or wireless devices. They think we're criminals or something. It's a significant hurdle to get over. So are the distractions; my writing space is in full view of a guard tower and a dozen other cells, on a zone where the worst prisoners in MDOC are housed, on High Risk in a building with Death Row. The atmosphere is an incessant booming of chaos. I've written fiction while fires burned in front of cells, toilet water covered the zone floor, flooded by inmates at war with the prison staff. I've written while K-9 officers tore through cells during shakedowns, pepper spray in the air. I see people post images of their writing spaces, cozy offices with tranquil views of nature, and wonder if I could sit down in a quiet spot like that and write anything. Would it be too easy?

GRAHAM MASTERSON (*The Manitou*): I write at home in a quiet room (but facing the street, so I can be nosey and see what's going on in the neighborhood). I don't listen to music when I write, because I believe that writing that is involving and easy to read needs simplicity and rhythm, and I don't want Beethoven's rhythms influencing mine. I write every day, even if I don't particularly feel like it. When you work for a newspaper or a magazine, you can't tell your editor that you have writer's block. In fact, I used to think that writer's block was a building where all these writers sat staring at blank sheets of paper and didn't have a clue what to write. I start the day with one very strong coffee. Then I just write until I come to a natural break in the story—sometimes three pages, sometimes ten. Then I go to the pub and meet my girlfriend.

ELKA RAY (*Saigon Dark*): I work on a big covered porch overlooking my garden in Central Vietnam. This is also where my family eats and hangs out. As well as writing fiction, I edit and illustrate. My workdays start around 8 a.m., after my kids leave for school. I typically work through lunch until 3:30 or 4, and then I head to the ocean for a swim.

A lot of people think working at home means you're not really working. While I wish books wrote themselves, mine don't, dammit.

EDDIE GENEROUS (*Radio Run*): My process has changed over the years. I used to write more than 700,000 words a year (most of those haven't been published). I needed to get those words out, writing every day, beating the bad out of my fingers and head, maybe, hopefully. Two million words or so is a good building block to have beneath you as a writer. For me, it was a must because my arc to publishable was slow.

Anyway, I did that for about three years, but I've since settled into 200,000 to 300,000 words a year because I've come to understand what I'm capable of and what's worth doing. Nobody publishes 700,000 words in a year and has readers for all those words anyway. If I find homes for half of what I write, I'm pretty happy with it. (That's a lie. I'd like to sell everything, and it irks the hell out of me when I can't find homes for stuff I think is good. But I can live with half.)

I write or edit something personal every week, and when I'm getting down to a longer piece, I need to get it out as quickly as possible, so a novella usually takes a week or ten days, a novel is usually a month or less. But I give myself the time, shut out the rest of the world, because usually, I've put in long days preceding and have afforded myself the time.

BRIAN BARR (*Dark Ripple: When Lovecraft Met Crowley*): I have a free-flow intuitive approach to storytelling, which can be note-heavy but never dominated by strict outlines. I like to write as the story comes, and I'm often coming up with more ideas as I write.

JOHN W. WOOD (*White Crow*): When I get into a story, I will have that story buzzing around in my head always. I'll wake up at 5:30 in the morning having conversations with my characters. I make a pot of coffee, pour a cup, go to my recliner in the bedroom, kick back and grab my laptop. I am of no use to anyone from that moment on for at least three hours. My wife will begin to stir, and I will go and make her a cup of tea and pour myself a cup of coffee. We talk about what I've written and about our plans for the day. An hour later, I'm back to writing for another three to four hours. Phone conversations with a honey-do thrown in get me out of my chair and moving around so I don't get gangrene of the legs. With that said, there may be days in a row when I don't write a thing, I work around the house, or the wife and I go out and enjoy our retirement. At a restaurant, my wife will often say, "Hey, tell your friends to go home, you talk to me." We laugh, and I come back to the party.

G. MIKI HAYDEN (*Strings*): When I'm writing, I write in my second bedroom, which I call my office, for as many hours a day as I have left between my practices of various types, my teaching online at *Writer's Digest*, and my private line-editing service—which is now under heavy demand. I also fritter away a bit of time. So then, that's when I write.

JENNIFER BROWN (*Hate List*): Fortunately, I am one of those people who can stop, drop, and write anywhere. Most often, I am in the chair in my living room with my laptop balanced on my lap, or at my kitchen table, writing while making dinner or doing some other chore. But I've been known to write in airports, hotels, airplanes, the back seats of taxis, at the neighborhood pool, coffee shops, libraries, teachers' lounges, etc. Because I do a lot of school visits, I do a lot of traveling, so I have to be adaptable or I would lose a lot of writing time. I also have to work around a part-time library job, so I have to be flexible with my schedule. But I started my writing adventure when I still had two preschoolers in my house, so I cut my teeth on flexibility. It's second nature to me now.

I do try to write every day, and I do try to write at least 1,000 words per day. But there are days when I spend all my "writing time" working on a website issue or answering emails or filling out interviews or working on social media and marketing and write zero words. I balance those days by having 5,000-word days whenever I can. I tend to mentally burn out after 5,000 words, so I try not to go over that.

DAVID CLARK (*Game Master*): I write four days a week, anywhere between 1,500-2,000 words each session. I don't have a special place for writing yet. It is usually just me and my laptop in the living room.

SAMANTHA BRYANT (*Face the Change: Menopausal Superheroes*): When I turned forty-two—which, as we all know, is the meaning of life, the universe, and everything (thanks, Douglas Adams!)—I decided it was time to give this writing thing a real go and stop futzing around. Up until then, I wrote haphazardly, when I felt inspired. As a result, I began thousands of stories and projects only to let them fizzle out when the initial rush of excitement petered out. I'd been writing for most of my life and had a handful of small publications to show for it. Unimpressive.

So, in my forty-second year, I committed to a daily writing habit. I found an online community and a spreadsheet tool called The Magic Spreadsheet, which gamified the process, giving me points for hitting my goal each day and letting me level up, setting the goal higher when I got better at it. It took a few fits and starts—I struggled at first to make even the 250 word a day minimum—but eventually, I became a daily writer.

My chain of days-in-a-row-on-which-I-wrote is now over four years long (though of course, I'm still just forty-two years old and will be as long as I can get people to buy that). My daily goal is now 850 words, and many days I double that. There's a bit of a seasonal swing to my word count, too—I produce more on school holidays and summer vacation because more of my day is my own to plan and use as I choose. But I always write, every day. Sick or well, come hell or high water.

CHRIS MILLER (*A Murder of Saints*): I have a goal to write every day, but with my current work and family schedule (full-time job and a wife and three kids all under nine years old), it just doesn't happen. I have three specified times a week that I'm able to nail down to do some writing, and then I squeeze in more when I can. Four to five days a week is typically what I manage. I also need a relatively quiet environment. I can't listen to music, even instrumental music, because it distracts me. Some minor background noise is fine, but people talking to me or TV or radio on, and it shuts me down.

But my overall process is this: an idea forms, sometimes several. I let them brew for a while, growing in my mind, and characters start to form, but vaguely still at that point. Then, after the basic premise is formed in my mind, along with a few characters, I try to think of where the story should begin. Then I sit down at the computer and floor it. I don't outline. I've tried, and all it did was to stifle my creative flow. So I just write and see where the story goes. I'm always surprised where I end up, but so far it's been a great place. Once the rough draft is done, I let it sit at least a few weeks and I work on something else, write a few short stories, what have you. Then, after it's fermented a while, I start going back through it.

MAX ALLAN COLLINS (*Road to Peridition*): My office is filled with framed art, shelves of favorite books, shelves of DVDs and Blu-rays, and other pop culture. The art is original comic art, pin-up originals, and cover paintings of Spillane stuff and my own books. I like having all of that creativity around me. I tend to do business in the morning and write in the afternoon and, if I didn't get my quota—currently ten finished pages, though it used to be a finished chapter no matter the length—I work again starting around 9 p.m. I write six days a week, and make sure to take a day off. My wife Barb, also a writer and my collaborator on the *Antiques* cozy mystery series, and I take a break between books for a brief getaway for shopping, movies, and general relaxation.

THOMAS GUNTHER (*The Big Book of Bootleg Horror: Volume Four*): I write when I can or when I can make time to write. Like many writers, I have a day job. And family. And a dog. And problems. Finding time is the biggest part of my process. The second one is finding peace and quiet. Fortunately, I have my own office here in my home (when we moved here, I insisted I got one of the rooms for an office). Normal, everyday noises don't bother me too much. I can usually tune them out. But loudness, like screaming kids, or drunken, boisterous neighbors, proves difficult. I need some headphones. That would help. So, I often write in spurts, usually early in the morning, when the rest of the world is fairly still. I can write in a restaurant or coffee shop, but I don't own a laptop, and my hands cramp too easily working the old-fashioned way with pen and paper. Sometimes I can work in a library, though. But most times, I work from right here in my den. I know some writers need music to get them motivated. Occasionally I listen to music, but even that can prove distracting. I guess it depends on my mood.

JOHN PALISANO (*Night of 1,000 Beasts*): Currently, most of my writing time is taken during very short periods. Several minutes can add up quickly if you've been thinking of a scene for half a day. Thankfully, the smart phones are great for producing easily editable text on the go. Waiting to pick up my kid at school. Doctor's office. A few moments before a client. It's helped my productivity from completely stalling. I average maybe 500-1,000 words a day. It takes discipline to budget my breaks and waiting time for storytelling instead of other distractions, but the stories need to come out or they'd likely kill me!

MAXWELL BAUMAN (*The Anarchist Kosher Cookbook*): I write a little bit every day. Some days I only write 500 words, other days I reach 2,000 to 3,000 words. Although I have higher daily word counts when working on the first drafts, because I'm just letting everything flow. When I'm working at home, I write best first thing in the morning or right before bed. I also feel like I can get a lot done when I'm writing on a bus or a plane, because then I can tune everything else out and focus on the story. Speaking of tunes, I also come up with a playlist of songs related to the piece that are either directly connected to the themes or events or find something that evokes a certain tone.

BEV VINCENT (*Flight or Fright*): I write every weekday from about 5:30 to 7:30 a.m. On weekends, I sometimes get nothing done, a little done, or a lot, depending on what else is going on. I have an upstairs office with a roll-top desk, which is where I do most of my writing. My computer is on a "kangaroo" platform that allows me to work standing up or sitting down, depending on my mood.

My other favorite writing environment is at the local café, where I take a journal and handwrite while I have breakfast and tea. Many of my first drafts these days—especially when writing fiction—are done longhand. I then dictate the story into the computer and do all subsequent work electronically. I also do a lot of off-line revision at the café.

I usually listen to music when I'm working on the first draft of something, but edit and revise in silence. I rarely object to interruptions; I can put something down and pick it back up again later without losing the thread. I'm the same way with reading—I can put a book down in the middle of a sentence if someone asks me something or I have to go somewhere.

I don't really keep track of how much I write on any given day. Sometimes "writing" involves something other than putting words down on the page. Researching something for a story, for example, which takes time but doesn't contribute to word count directly. There are also a lot of other things involved in the writing business—reviewing and signing contracts, signing signature sheets for limited editions, reviewing proofs, responding to interview questions, etc. It all has to get done during that limited amount of time I have for "writing."

PAUL D. BRAZILL (*Cold London Blues*): My approach to writing is pretty much my approach to the rest of my life—ad hoc and slapdash. I write pretty much when I feel like it. I stop when I lose interest or have something else to do. Sometimes I listen to music. Sometimes I have the TV on. Sometimes silence. There's no consistency to it, for sure. Thankfully

I'm not a professional writer—looking at them moaning on social media, they seem to lead a life of abject misery!

TRAVIS WALLACE (*Clues*): Since I don't get to enjoy, or am not brave enough to enjoy, a full-time writing process, I am not very regimented until I believe I have something and I need to get it finished. I write a lot on planes and in restaurants and bars while on the road for my regular job. On mornings when I don't have obligations (kids, work, honey-dos), I like to sit on my front porch when doing longhand (always my first draft) or at my architect-style desk when typing (second draft and beyond), looking out the big bay window of my home office.

When I was to a point I was going to make my first book happen, I became more structured, and my family allowed me the space to do so. I worked over my lunch period, I worked three nights a week for two to four hours each night, and I worked on weekends for two to three hours every morning. The nights got late and mornings got early because my friend insomnia would eventually set in. Towards the end, my late nights and early mornings started to overlap.

PAUL HEATLEY (*An Eye for an Eye*): I make sure to write every day, in some capacity. Whether that be planning, editing, proof-reading, or actually writing itself. Writing is a muscle that has to be exercised, and I prefer to exercise it daily. If I'm actually writing something, I like to aim for 1,000 words a day, though sometimes in the early phases, getting into the swing of things, it can be just 500, but I don't like to keep that going for too long, I'd far rather be doing 1,000.

My writing tends to be done late at night, roughly between the hours of nine and eleven. I'm at work during the day, and I have other commitments, so night time is best for me, though on days off I'll write whenever I get the chance and give myself a rare night off—but only providing something has already been done. I've got a desk in my bedroom. I recently tidied it up, because it used to be a total mess with notebooks and scraps of paper. It's actually quite neat now. I also invested in some sticky tags, which mark where I've planned stuff in certain notebooks, so that helps me keep track of things. The wall above my desk is covered in posters, postcards, and pictures. It's got The Doors, Jack Kerouac, Clint Eastwood, Rocky, Blondie, James Dean, Marilyn Monroe, Marlene Dietrich, and others. Oh, and it also has a tweet sent to me by Mark Lanegan that I printed out where he says he enjoyed my book *Fatboy*.

So yeah, I make sure to do something every day. I saw something once that said "Every day you don't write is a day you've wasted." I feel that, I feel it hard. If I'm not working in some capacity, I feel irritable and antsy. When I got into the swing of writing every day, it really evened me out. If I'm not working, everything feels like wasted effort.

BRIAN JAMES LANE (*Fright Feast*): I write many ideas down. I make a lot of notes (some of which contradict each other) when developing a novel outline. These ideas usually take me longer to navigate than the actual writing does. I'm sure there's a better way, but this is just how I'm wired. I need to sift through the mass of projectile vomiting of my unfettered and unarranged musings. It ain't a great system, but it's mine.

I tend to write better in the early morning. Forcing myself to lose sleep is best for productivity. If I must get up, then it better be worth it! Coffee helps, too. I may have more "free time" at the end of the day, but by then, I am wiped and don't feel like being creative. It takes a lot of effort to write or even think about writing. I don't think people who aren't creative truly understand that. It's effort, and best done when you have proper energy for it.

The environment itself varies, but making it an event is important. You get a sense of professionalism by leaving the house. I have written in libraries, shops, planes, and even a laundromat to great success. Comfort breeds laziness. I think it helps to get out and go someplace. This sends your brain the message that you are going to work, not simply plugging away lackadaisically on a hobby. When I do write at home, I like to do it in the basement in an uncomfortable chair. This is out of my comfort zone and helps me to focus on the work.

CARMEN AMATO (*Cliff Diver*): I have a dedicated office at home and write almost every day. Despite the nice workspace, there are a distractions like the ever-needy dog, and I love writing in a spiral notebook in a coffee shop or the local library.

PAUL TREMBLAY (*Head Full of Ghosts*): I generally write in the dining room, which I've taken over as a makeshift office. But I also write at school if I have free periods. I've written in gymnasiums while waiting for my kids' sport ball practice to end as well. Have laptop, will travel. Having a full-time job and being a full-time parent is a good lesson in time management, or taking advantage of time, might be a better description. I write when and where I can.

I typically write 400 to 500 words a day when I'm going well. I give myself permission to miss a day or two if life is busy. That word count can take anywhere from forty-five minutes to two hours. The word count doesn't sound like much, but it adds up.

LILY LAMB (*The Dowling House*): I tend to write after midnight and in cafes. I write on my laptop. It's always in my bag, and most of the tables have a power-point so I can just sit as long as I want. I order my coffee and muffin and just enjoy myself. I write a lot depending on how crushed I get due to poor sales.

CHARLES LYNNE (*What Screams in the Dark*): I try to write something, anything, every day. Whether it's a short story, a poem, or on my novel. Typically, I'm sitting in my recliner with my Chromebook in my lap. I use Google docs for saving and sharing. Google docs also allows me to continue writing no matter where I am and no matter what device I'm using, be it laptop, Chromebook, or even a cell phone.

MIKE PURFIELD (*In a Blackened Sky Where Dreams Collide*): I write Monday through Friday, 2,000 words a day. Weekends, I try to sneak in some, but if I don't, that's okay. My goal is 40,000 words a month on a novel. I don't outline. I have a sense of where I am going or what points to hit. Primarily, I am a creative writer. I sit down with the characters, pop in a conflict, and let them achieve their goal, and I figure it out as I go along.

ISOBEL BLACKTHORN (*Clarissa's Warning*): With the exception of forced breaks when I am caught up with book promotion or traveling, I write every day, starting from the moment I wake. I do not want anything to interfere with those precious moments when I steer myself towards my writing, pick up the pen and set to. I usually have a long break after a few hours and deal with admin, then I go back and spend a few more hours composing. I am not a hugely productive author. I write between one to three thousand words a day. They are words that have been handwritten and then typed up and edited a bit.

BOB VAN LAERHOVEN (*Return to Hiroshima*): I have been a full-time author over here in Belgium/Flanders for more than twenty-five years. All that time I tried to push and punch some punctuality in my writing. I never succeeded.

In hindsight, I can see favorite periods: for weeks/months on end, I wrote between 5 a.m. and 8 a.m. Then, for no apparent reason, the rhythm changed, and I worked mostly during the afternoon or in the evening. I have had writing periods between 3 a.m. and 6 a.m., and so on....

Divorces usually mean that one of the partners is moving on. Fate dictated that I was that partner, so I have written in several houses or apartments. It's hard to pick a place that felt exceptionally good out of that list. I think I always forgot my surroundings when I was working on my novels. Physically, I sat behind my computer, but my mind was coasting along the settings of my stories, feeling at home there.

HEYWOOD GOULD (*Fort Apache, The Bronx*): I try to write at least five days a week, five hours a day. Sometimes, I get a sixth day in. I hate vacations and holidays, because my schedule is thrown off. I work in the nearest public library. Occasionally, I'll wander around the stacks and pick out a book at random, finding some writer I never heard of who is a lot better than me.

DAVID L. TAMARIN (*BOLO: Sociopaths on a Rampage*): I write a lot, but not on a schedule. Normally, I write when I have free time, which is a lot, unless I am in the middle of something good, and then I drop everything and write. I've learned to write on my iPhone, so I'm always writing. At traffic lights, in line at the store, I can write because of apps on my smart phone. Even if I go to work, I can write that way. I also use my iPad, which is easier because it's bigger, but I don't always have it with me. I'll write in any environment, but I prefer my gloomy basement at home. It's the biggest mess. I can't keep a clean writing space. Not if my life depended on it.

BRET MCCORMICK (*Headhunters from Outer Space*): Behavioral psychologists tell us most of what we do and most of our emotions are hard-wired responses built on the foundation of avoiding pain and moving toward pleasure. After decades of alcohol and drug abuse, I got clean and sober in March of 2014. That's when my writing became a serious endeavor rather than a sporadic hobby. I pretty much write every day. Taking a cue from the behaviorists, I have linked writing with my one remaining vice—caffeine. I have my first cup of coffee in the morning, meditate, and as I grab my second cup, I begin writing. The pleasant mood-enhancing effects of the dark brew in conjunction with pecking on the keys of my laptop has turned the process of writing into my greatest pleasure. Never a chore. Perhaps an addiction. Writing is something I want (maybe need) to do every day. I crouch against the headboard of our huge, high bed (we call it the dog-free plateau, because it's the only place in the house we are safe from the relentless affection of our four small dogs) with the laptop across my legs, and I knock out 3,000 words, sometimes more. I like it quiet. By that, I mean no music. In a house with four dogs and four birds, it's never completely quiet.

AUTUMN CHRISTIAN (*Girl Like a Bomb*): I wake up like a bomb has gone off in the middle of the night and frantically try to reassemble the pieces. Then when I feel human again, I get to work. Most of the time, I work from home, but lately, I've been going to Starbucks with my laptop. (Their black coffee always seems to have a lingering burnt taste, so you usually have to get something with flavored syrup for it to be palatable. I'd rather go somewhere local, but this is currently my only option at the moment.) Write for a few hours until I get hungry, and then go home and take care of some chores. It's been easier to write without the endless distractions of a home with three dogs in it and getting it done first thing in the morning. Going to a coffee shop with a purpose seems to keep me on task much better as well.

It's hard being both the animal and the whip that drives it.

I am a person with a high-conscientiousness score (Google big five personality test and take it if you haven't! It changed a lot about how I understand myself.), so I'm always sort of doing something. I'm really only happy when I'm working, or my rest feels well-deserved. I try to write or do some kind of work related to writing whenever I can. I also take a lot of pictures for my social media. (Hey, that's work, right?! I'm a millennial, if I'm not on the Internet, do I even exist?). I used to have a word count of 1,000 that I tried to reach every day, but I gave that up. It's not so much the words as the quality of work. And so many days are just priming me for when I can actually hit high word counts.

KURT BELCHER (*Spiders & Stardust*): I write every day, to one degree or another. Sometimes it's a drawing day (I write and draw comics), so it might only be a little. But any time writing is good time writing, I think. Even if it's just researching scripts, moving ideas around, or just brainstorming ideas and characters. Process is varied for me, though. It's rarely writing an idea fully-formed. It can also be a few unrelated ideas that just happen to cluster together. More often, though, it's a reverse onion sort of thing, where I start with a kernel of an idea, and build from there until I get an outline with enough meat on it to start writing. From there, it sticks to the general outline I wrote, but I also try to do things that surprise even me. I can write anywhere, but as with most writers, seclusion is probably ideal. I do like to have some music playing while I work, but nothing you'd sing along to.

KASEY PIERCE (*Pieces of Madness*): Boredom is a luxury, and "downtime" doesn't exist in my world. When I punch out from the day job, the writer takes over and savors every minute I have to be that writer. That's the tough thing about being in a writer's life. We always seem as if we're shutting people out or penciling them in. That's just how it is, though. Our lives are one big schedule. It's manna from heaven when we find a few hours of silence and isolation. So my answer to "how much do you write" is "as much as possible." I can't say anything beyond that.

Speaking of silence and isolation, if the environment isn't a mortuary, it sucks. Silence won't always be available, though. That's why headphones are a necessity. From my perspective, reading and writing is about traveling—visiting different times, places, even realms in your mind. Music really helps to set the tone. Nothing gives your writing a soundtrack…like a soundtrack. For instance, Basil Poledouris' *Conan the Barbarian* is one of my absolute favorites when writing something of epic proportions.

DEV JARRETT (*Loveless*): I try to write at least a thousand words a day when I'm writing. Some days, I simply know I won't be able to write (family time, working longer hours at the day job, traveling: you know, life). When the words and ideas are coming together more quickly, sometimes I write more. A key strategy for me is not beating myself up over not being able to write for a day or two in a row—we all make those choices, and we have to live with those choices. We all have to maintain a balance of the elements of our lives, and spending too much time inside our own heads can be counterproductive.

Thankfully, the writing environment is a moveable feast these days. Take the laptop anywhere, plug in my earbuds, and dive in. That said, I usually end up writing either at an actual desk or sitting on my sofa in the living room. I've written in tents in the Afghan desert, and I've written in underground bunkers on islands in the Pacific. Wherever *you* are, that's where your fiction factory is.

MELISSA KEIR (*Cowboy, Mine*): I am a pantser, so I write without an outline. I sit down at my computer and start at the beginning of the story and end with the happily ever after.

The characters speak to me. I see them in mind, what they are doing and what their lives are like. I spend some time wondering what would happen if they did one thing or another, and then I add them to my story. Times when I'm driving, walking along the lake shore, or in the shower are wonderful for creating that movie in my head.

If I'm not currently working on a story, but I have characters who are talking, I will put down a beginning of their manuscript so I don't forget it.

I like to write in the evenings. I have a laptop, so I will climb into bed with the dogs and snuggle up to write. I try to get about 1,000 words done each evening before I put the computer away. Usually there isn't any noise, and the lights are low, which provides me with a soothing environment, free of stress and distractions.

DAVID OWAIN HUGHES (*Brain Damage*): I try to write every day, with a minimum word count of 1,000 words in mind. Failing that, anything will do, as long as I get something down. I tell myself to "get my arse in that chair and produce, and don't think of coming out of that office until you've done some work, you worthless maggot." My muse is a terrifying dominatrix—I'm just glad she doesn't have a hold over my wedding tackle.

Another thing: I never work on more than one project at a time. I like to give one piece of work my full attention. If ideas strike, I jot them down and keep moving. In my opinion, you shouldn't distract yourself. You wouldn't screw another person behind your current lover's back, would you? If no, then don't cheat on your work-in-progress, palooka. Make it feel special.

My writing environment is dusty, colorful, chaotic, and cluttered—the total opposite of how I am as a person. Maybe that's how it works, ya know? Like cat people shouldn't marry dog people, but they do, and it clicks. Amidst the disorder, I've surrounded myself with things that make me happy: photos of my children and gorgeous fiancée, my published titles, pop vinyls, movie memorabilia, the novels I love, etc.

JEFF PARSONS (*The Captivating Flames of Madness*): I do technical writing at work, so I get lots of practice making up stories. Yep, I tell some whoppers here and there. It's all about perspective. To me, writing isn't about sitting down on a swivel chair before a computer monitor and typing out a finished story in one breathless moment. The idea has to grow into something interesting to me or else I get bored. Once you get an idea, it has to be integrated into a real-life world scenario or something close to that (if you can fake it). I start crafting words after I've figured out the skeleton for a decent story. Kind of like building a house: foundation, framework, roof, plywood walls, electrical, plumbing, drywall, and so on, and plenty of inspectors, and when that's done, the crazy cat lady can move in. A simple outline helps me, just to help keep it logical before I even begin. I used to hate creating an outline more than getting a colonoscopy, but eventually, I learned that an outline (not the colonoscopy) is less work in the long run and it helps you to avoid agonizing plot inconsistencies. I avoid terrifying writing situations like "Hey, weren't you dead in the previous chapter?" Then, after a colonoscopy, er, outline, I add details for scene descriptions. After that gets sorted out, I go back and add personal character touches, so I'm probably more plot-driven at first, then I dive in deep with the emotions. I recommend finding a good writers-critique group, one where the people don't just talk in useless generalities (so… this writing… here and here and here… it needs to be more boring…). A good group actually writes down alternative ways for you to say something. And their treatment of your story is honestly critical, but kind and encouraging. Then, off I go to dabble in more rewrites to fine tune the story.

I can do writing work in almost any environment. I wasn't always that way, but learned how to do it (and, wow, that took a while). I'm glad, too—I wouldn't want to limit myself. New environments also spark different types of creativity and while not all of them are very efficient, the work does get done. I get different ideas working in a busy coffee shop than I do at home in the perfect quiet stillness. You have to figure out what makes you happy.

MICHAEL CIESLAK (*Desolation: 21 Tales for Tails*): I would love to say that I have a dedicated time where I sit down and write every day. Unfortunately, that is not the case. Between the day job, family, and the publishing work, I'll take any opportunity to write that I can. This often means writing in tiny bits and pieces in weird places. I'll frequently take breaks in my car to get in twenty minutes of writing. At my old job, I would lock myself in the supply closet so I could get a little peace and quiet (which meant occasionally scaring the crap out of the secretary when she came looking for Post-It-Notes or staples).

I'm also a big fan of writing in public, but very rarely in coffee shops. For some reason, the noise in coffee shops intrudes into my head. I find it much easier to write in bars. The music and voices in bars become a nice white noise that is the perfect ambient sound to write in. Writers write in bars; coffee shops are for poets.

PHIL PRICE (*Unknown*): This is where it gets interesting. I don't really have a set process. I have a full-time day job and a young family, which takes up almost all of my time. I normally write at the dining table, whilst supervising the chaotic antics of my boys. If I am in the zone, I can blast out 5,000 words a weekend, which for me is good. My perfect environment is at the dining table, in an empty house with Alexa playing soothing tunes.

JESSE DEDMAN (*The Master's Torment*): The hardest part is the blank page. I sit in the chair and stare at it, while searching for the right way to open the story. Want something that gripes, but don't want it to be cliché. I'll spend about twenty minutes on this, no joke. The rest just flows in.

JAMES WATTS (*Them*): I generally sit down at my computer desk, go to YouTube, and select the music that best fits the genre I am writing in. In my case, it's mostly horror. So, I will listen to dark music with hardly any vocals. I try to write every day when not fighting stress.

A.P. SESSLER (*The First Suitor*): Since I work in so many mediums, the best way to get in the writing zone is to do the cliché sit at the coffee shop (so screw you, Family Guy!). Yes, I'm that surly-looking dude seated at the counter staring at his laptop. For inspiration, might I plug Darren Charles' Unearthing Forgotten Horrors online radio show? It's a wonderful mix of horror soundtracks, prog folk, doom blues, noise, and really keeps me going. I do this four hours twice a week.

When I get home, I marry the new material to the old and rarely keep going, because once I'm in front of my desktop, I usually work on art, animation, or music.

JASON PARENT (*A Life Removed*): I like absolute silence. When I write, a movie of the story is playing in my head, so that I am more or less just putting into words that which I am envisioning. Distractions are more than annoyances; they take me right out of the scene.

STANLEY B. WEBB (short-story writer, numerous anthologies): I experience long periods without writing, or doing any other creative work, then have productive phases. Sometimes, the theme of a new market inspires me. When I start a story, I tend to work on it until completion. Then, if the market's deadline allows, I take a break before I edit.

Before my retirement, I wrote while at work between the cycles of the machine that I operated. Now, I do all of my writing at home. Whether I write in longhand or on the computer, I prefer to sit at a table. (When I was young, I usually wrote while I lounged on the sofa, or balanced my typewriter on my lap.)

WADE H. GARRETT (*Pigs: An Extreme Horror Novella*): Since I have a full-time job, I get about one to two hours a day to write. I usually write in my living room on a laptop.

RICHARD CHRISTIAN MATHESON (*Scars and Other Distinguishing Marks*): Deadlines help to move things along. I tend to write fast, having spent many years as a writer/producer where production demands are a constant.

ANDREW LENNON (*Bound*): I don't write as often as I'd like. When I'm in the zone, I can easily write a few thousand words a day, usually just in an hour or two. The problem is I have many slumps in which I can go weeks at a time without writing anything at all. I almost always write in bed, as I find it easier to lose myself in the story if I'm locked away from everyone and everything. I just have my old horror movies playing and then drift away into my own mind.

PEGGY CHRISTIE (*Hell Hath No Fury*): I'm not sure I have a process. I *cannot* force myself to write every day. I just can't. When I do that, I don't enjoy it anymore. Then I get very, very angry, and the next thing I know, I'm standing in the middle of town with blood on my hands, all my clothes shredded, and I get banned from public gatherings.

I usually write when I'm in the mood, but I can force myself to work when I know it's necessary (usually a deadline or I've been lazy for too long.) And I write until I get stuck or my eyes cross, whichever happens first. Most of the time, I write out a story longhand, usually because I'm not at my computer. I keep a lot of dedicated notebooks for certain projects, but I also have a bunch of blank ones around the house so I can write anything that sparks in my brain.

I don't outline, but I will write down major plot points or any ideas I want to address in a story so I won't forget them. I can't listen to music, though. I end up creating dance routines in my head instead of writing.

CHRISTOPH PAUL (*A Confederacy of Hot Dogs*): I am an editor as much as I am an author, but I can't write much after I edit others. So I try to write early and then do "work," which is editing and publishing others. There are three places I like to write: on my porch when the weather is nice, at a coffee house/library, but my favorite place seems to be in a room with a TV on. I like atmosphere for certain projects so I'll put on a TV show to feed off that energy.

BILLY CHIZMAR (*Widow's Point*): Being a full-time college student and student-athlete means that I don't get to do as much writing as I'd like to. I make time for it on a weekly basis and when a hot idea strikes, but it's a struggle. As such, I have to scrap for my writing time and get it in wherever and whenever I can. I even wrote a couple of stories on the bus to and from away games last year. The only constant is that I'm always listening to some music, genre usually varying depending on the tone of the story.

JOE X. YOUNG (short-story writer, numerous anthologies): I try to write every day, which isn't always possible. I have just finished NaNoWriMo, which was difficult as we have a houseguest who stays with us the last week in November and first week in December, so it's hardly a great environment to have the peace and quiet required to focus on bashing out a few thousand words of pure gold every day, so sometimes I'm lucky if I can manage a few hundred words of tin. This year was doubly difficult, as I already have multiple disabilities, but more recently my right index fingertip tore a tendon; it's not repairable and is hooked and twisted for life. Okay, not painful, but I'm no longer hitting the keys with accuracy. It'll take some training before it becomes useful again. I can also add that my arms are both in medical supports as I have calcific tendinitis in both shoulders and had my first shock wave therapy treatment today. Altogether I lost two weeks of November to illness, and another was dented by the houseguest. However, I have still hit my NaNoWriMo target of 50,000 words and am continuing to write the story beyond that, as there's a much bigger book in it than 50k can do justice to.

In essence, I write what I can when I can, and will do my best to overcome any obstacle, because to me, writing is that important and I love it. Daily word counts? Not interested in that so much. I set a 2,000 words a day count for NaNoWriMo and failed a lot, but kicked its ass in the end, so it's all about perseverance paying off with that end goal of actually having written a story.

DEAN M. DRINKEL (*Demonologica Biblica*): I am a full-time creative and am currently working across a number of mediums (and genres). I will make sure that every day as a minimum I hit at least 1,000 words (on a story or novella) or ten pages on a film script. If I have a number of stories or scripts on the go (which, to be honest, I usually do), then I ensure that I work on everything every day. I'm usually up early and will attend to social media first before then hitting a project and will continue to about 9 a.m. when I have breakfast. I'm trying to improve my French-speaking skills (as I live most of the time in France—though this year has been a bit more in the UK because of some TV scripts I was working on), so that will be an hour or so before I then work on projects until 1-ish and take a break for lunch. I'll check emails and social media until about 3 p.m. before the afternoon slog; I'll break then about 5:30 for another French lesson and dinner. There's a soap opera I'm a little obsessed with right now, so I'll watch that early in the evening before doing a final hour or two. The way my brain works is that I need all these projects going on at once—I can get a little bored if I just concentrate on one at a time—so it's all doable for me.

EVANS LIGHT (*Black Door*): "Get it done first, make it perfect later" has become my new mantra, and it's done wonders for my productivity. I have it printed and hung up in both of my writing areas.

I listen to non-distracting rhythmic music while composing first drafts. Over the years, I've developed a collection of albums that are about forty-five minutes long and really help to get me in the zone. When whatever album I'm playing ends, I call it quits and wrap up the writing session. I usually edit in silence, though, to be able to better hear the cadence of prose and dialogue.

I tire after about forty-five minutes of consistent writing, during which I can typically produce about 500 words of new text. Rarely, I'll find myself so inspired by a project that I'll write from one sunrise to the next, but I try not to do that often, as it leaves me spent and in pain, causing me to cringe at the thought of writing anything else for some time after. A solid hour per day spent writing or editing is satisfactory for me. Then again, I'm not a prolific author.

JAMES H. LONGMORE (*Pede*): I write just about every day, in a quiet room (far too easily distracted!), and I set myself a word target—a happy throwback from my previous career in sales, I'm still obsessively target-oriented—and hit the keys until I've achieved that target, be it good or bad.

There are many authors I know who go back and polish their work as they go along, but I find it better for me to plough on to the end *before* attempting any editing/polishing—if I did not, I would no doubt end up with an incredibly well-edited and beautifully-polished quarter of a book and nothing else!

And then it's back to the beginning again! Hemingway, between slugs of gut-rot whiskey, is credited with saying "writing is rewriting", which is pretty damn accurate! It's the part of the job that most of us hate—why, oh why, can't our novels turn out just perfect on the first draft!?—and it may take three, four, or more edits before it's anything near ready to be seen by the great reading public!

MEGAN O'RUSSELL (*Girl of Glass*): My non-writing career is as a professional actor in musical theatre, so my schedule and writing environment changes a lot based on what contract I'm doing and where.

For example, I was on the 2017-2018 North American Tour of *The Wizard of Oz*. During those months, I spent a lot of time working in my seat on the tour bus and backstage at the show. When I'm in a show that doesn't travel, I tend to write in my room in cast housing on whatever surface (quite often a lap desk) is available.

When my life isn't utterly insane with rehearsals or travel, I try to write 2,000—2,500 words a day when I'm not editing, and 1,000 words a day if I am. I aim for writing six days a week (a standard theatre work week), but again, life happens, and I won't beat myself up about missing a day to take some time for maintaining my sanity.

ANDREW BUCKLEY (*Hair in All the Wrong Places*): I have a fairly hectic family life: wife, three kids, two dogs, a full-time writing job, speaking engagements, travel, etc. I lack time. I'd like to be able to either clone myself (as long as it isn't an evil clone . . . Wait, what if I'm the evil clone?) or master the art of time travel. Until then, I tend to write once everyone is in bed and asleep after 10 p.m. Most times, I write in bed, though I do have a home office (I just don't spend a lot of time there). As for frequency, it's whenever I can fit it in. When I write steadily, I aim for ten pages a week. If I'm on a deadline, it's as much as I can produce.

JOHN BODEN (*Jedi Summer with the Magnetic Kid*): My method is very slapdash. I don't outline or have a count in mind, Hell, oftentimes, all I've got is a character or a scene or image, and I just start typing and see what happens. I've got more folders of slivers and shards than complete stories.

LAURA ROBERTS (*Haiku for Lovers*): My writing methods vary, but typically I like to crank out as many words of my first draft in as short a time as possible. The shortest amount of time in which I've written a book is three days, during the Three Day Novel Contest. That laser focus of creative energy, poured out over seventy-two consecutive hours, is what finally got me to finish my first book. It's not a sustainable way to write books all the time, but it was a great way to get that particular story finished.

The general idea of writing so quickly is just to get the whole thing on paper so that I can see the story from A to Z. Then I can dig in and start scraping and sculpting it, slowly prodding that terrible first draft into something more polished. At first it's just about finishing the draft, and then it's all editing from there on out.

To me, the most important thing is keeping up the creative flow. If I'm not working on a book, I keep up a schedule of writing blog posts once a week, posting on social media daily, and journaling privately just to keep the momentum going.

ERIN SWEET AL-MEHAIRI (*Breathe, Breathe*): I really don't have a method. I'm a pantser, meaning I write by the seat of my pants. I write when inspiration strikes me, in the early mornings, sometimes when I wake from sleep with an idea, or in the car on a road trip, like on my napkin or something. My perfect idea of writing would be to write outside by the water or at a place of inspiration. I don't like routines and don't have one, nor do I worry about word counts, though I can say it might be good for someone who likes to make and achieve writing goals. I might try that in the future. When it comes to the next part of the process, editing, I carve out more focused time.

H.R. BOLDWOOD (*The Corpse Whisperer*): I call it the AIS method, better known as Ass in Seat. I allow myself to check my phone, Facebook, and e-mail one time before I begin writing. Then I cast them to the hinterlands until I break, usually at least a couple of hours later. Most days begin with a specific goal, but more often than not, the goal is not based on word count. It's usually connected to completion of specific scenes or a chapter. (I do track my word count, but just to keep an eye on my overall progress.) Each day starts with reviewing the prior day's work to ensure a seamless integration. I try to write daily, but sometimes life intrudes. And when it intrudes big time, I do my best to be patient with myself.

JULIA BRAMER (*The Vitamin D Treatment*): I try to write every day to keep in practice, even if there is no great inspiration (the muse), which I see as those first lines or thoughts that launch me. Once I've got something that feels alive with potential, I begin the work of crafting it. Many times I will find my structure, whether poetry or prose, echoing a Cabalistic form, which incorporates science, myth, and other layered meanings. (I'm into mysticism and read about this kind of stuff). A truly channeled piece can express multiple levels of meaning. I pare away the words that do nothing. If my work is a poem, I take a hard, critical look at all beginning and end words, knowing that such a prominent position is no place for a weak article. I try to remove all hints of cliche and everything that sounds remotely familiar and therefore unsurprising. Finally, I try to put it away for awhile, so that I can look at it with fresh, more critical eyes and see everything I missed the first few times.

RANDEE DAWN (*Home for the Holidays*): Often people speak of being a "pantser" or an "outliner" when it comes to organizing their storytelling; I've recently been told that in Europe, it's more "gardener" or "architect," which I like better. I have traditionally held the full story in my head, and written it out—no outline, no writing program other than Word. This last book came about after I'd outlined it for another medium and decided it wouldn't work in that format. I then realized it could be a novel, and I'd spent time actually creating an outline, which provided a safe scaffolding to create the first draft—I knew where I was going, if not always how I was getting there. I'm settling in to start my next book soon, and I'm not sure what I will do. Word count-wise, I don't worry about it until the story is finished. The story will tell you these things. Routine: I am a full-time freelance writer. I shove in time wherever possible, but I have sacred space between 7 to 9 each night during which I've told the husband "fire, flood, or blood" are the only reasons I can be interrupted.

LANNY LARCINESE (*I Detest All My Sins*): I begin with a character and give him a life-magnitude problem (e.g., guilt). I devise as I go. Often, he suggests his own backstory, tells me his needs, tells me what kind of girlfriend he wants, tells me what his problems are. Then I give him more problems. Then I give him more again and keep giving him more. I devise plot points which bring out the best and worst in him. I write by the seat of my pants. The story is never "finished," but at some point must be done. It is done when story questions are answered. I don't make it "over" as much as it becomes over. If not actually at the keyboard, I constantly think about the story, make random notes, run to the keyboard (at midnight if necessary) if I think of a good word, image, or plot point. I bang away at the keyboard when I'm in flow; other times lucky to get a couple hundred words down. I can seldom concentrate deeply for longer than two or three hours.

KATE JONEZ (*Lady Bits*): Being disciplined about writing is the hardest part. Setting a goal and giving myself rewards and punishments works for me. I like to give myself little trinkets for good writing sessions, and if I fail to make my daily word count—off with a finger. That'll teach me to complain about typing.

SCOTT M. GORISCAK (*Horrorism*): When I write, I don't allow anything to interfere with the content of an idea. I write until I exhaust my thoughts, then revisit the next day. I find that I'm more satisfied with my work if my thoughts flow naturally, rather than if I force myself to keep writing. So I write when I'm in the zone and don't let obstacles such as word counts dictate the story. The work is more important to me than the guidelines of a project. I would prefer to create a great story rather than something I feel is marginal just to collect a check.

ADRIENNE DELWO (*Hero Academy*): I don't have set writing times or anything like that, but when I'm actively writing, I'll usually put in between three and six hours a day. I set my word count goals and push myself to reach them. I approach writing like a job, in large part because I've written professionally for twenty-two years. Daily deadlines taught me that you don't wait for a muse—you just sit down and write. Every day won't be brilliant, but with fiction, you can always improve it later. You can't improve something you didn't write. I also don't have any rituals or requirements. I sit down and I write. Don't romanticize the process. Just write.

ESSELL PRATT (*Sharkantula*): When I start to write, the first paragraph seems to be the most difficult part, since it sets the immediate tone. For short stories, I go in blind and write what feels right. For books, I tend to outline first and then write. I don't worry about word count; instead I allow the story to pace itself. All too often, I see inexperienced writers place focus on word count or other items that reside outside of the actual story. I focus on the story first, then worry about the other details.

GEORGE LEA (*Strange Playgrounds*): I tend to start with an image or a sensation; much of my writing is visual or sensory by nature. I like immediacy in my work, so I tend to start with something that has aroused me in some way, be it an image, an idea, a line of argument, then scribble until something coalesces.

Many of my first drafts are hand-written (though my hand writing is appalling), as I find this helps to get them down far more immediately than if I sat in front of a keyboard. These first drafts tend to be emotive collections of images and ideas more than anything.

Then I type them out in more coherent form (though that's debateable), which is the point at which they either fail or become what they're meant to be. It's difficult expressing when or how that moment arrives; it's different for every tale, often idiosyncratic (some of the shorter stories in my first collection, *Strange Playgrounds,* were originally parts of much larger works, until I realized that the core of the story existed in one small part of the whole).

ERIC J. GUIGNARD (*That Which Grows Wild*): I try to write every day, even if it's only a dozen words. My personal goal is 1,000 words a day, though most writers I know strive for more, between 1,500—2,000. I always begin just by "writing as I go," but if the story becomes complicated or I get burned out or stuck, then I turn to outlining to figure the proper direction. I have no other rituals, except that I write when I can. I try to write in the morning after I wake up, the earlier the better. I also, oddly, have a time of greatest focus/ productivity in late afternoon. Our bodies cycle to rhythmic clocks and mine is set to pound out work at about 4:00 p.m. Of course, all that also depends on other work, family, and life obligations. I write technical documentation for my day job and also teach as adjunct U.C. faculty, and have two small children to raise, and volunteer with several organizations, so it's easy to let writing take a back seat to everything else, although I force myself to write something creative every single day, even if it's only fifty words or so.

MERCEDES M. YARDLEY (*Pretty Little Dead Girls*): I'm perhaps the most horrifically haphazard writer you'll come across. I try to write a little each day, but it's usually across a variety of projects. I'll work on this short story for half an hour. Then I'll switch to a script. I'll get up, walk around, and do some chores. I'll sit down to the short story again, then decide that I'd rather focus on a children's book. I answer e-mails. I read for anthologies or Shock Totem magazine. I work on my novel. So bits and pieces get done on each project, but nothing is done in a focused, timely manner. I'd like to streamline my process. My agent is having fits.

ROBERT FORD (*The God Beneath My Garden*): I tend to do a lot of internal research before really getting into a piece of work. At some point, I know how my main character will react in any given situation. If they were in a bank and it was getting robbed, I know whether they'll fight or give flight. I know how they'll flirt. What they drink, etc. A large portion of that may never make it into the actual work, but for me, it's very important so I truly know the character. It seems to work for me, because my reviews tend to mention characterization quite a lot. When I'm actually writing, it's always to music and that really depends on the piece—everything from Frank Sinatra to Nine Inch Nails. I try to get 500 to 1,000 words done at a clip, but also don't focus too much on the word count, but more on how it feels. Sometimes it's more because things are really buzzing along. Others, when it feels like pulling teeth, I just know it's not ready yet.

HOPE CLARK (*Murder on Edisto*): There's nothing complex about my writing method, which to me means I spend more energy in the creativity than the process. I take a simple lined notepad, brainstorm a section of the book with all options for the characters and plot, then sit down and see how many chapters I can milk out of it. Usually, the end result is three to five chapters. Repeat. I fight to write a minimum of 500 words and usually no more than 3,000 words per day. I'm not a binge writer. The faster I write, the less detailed and more unrealistic the writing, and those little nuances needed for voice don't appear as keen. Stories have to seep out of me, not gush. The writing I write fast and furious just isn't the quality as the words I pencil on paper, spin out on computer, then orally edit on my back porch. Yes, I edit as I go. Contrary to the lessons out there. The prouder I am of my writing as it evolves, the more I love to write, and the higher the quality of my work. So as a book evolves, the more I yearn to return to it. The editing, as I said, takes place on my back porch, reading aloud to my husband (who never reads, just loves to be read to), usually with a bourbon in hand. Sometimes we share a cigar. We face the lake, even take it into lunch and dinner on the porch. It's a ritual that's highly cherished in my house. It's one of my few processes, and if I've learned anything in twenty years of writing, it's that no two writers write alike, and that no teacher can tell you the best way.

W.B.J. WILLIAMS (*The Garden at the Roof of the World*): I write daily, but with breaks. I take weekends, I take holidays. I write at least 300 words a day. I'll write more to complete an idea, or scene. When I've completed a story I will give myself a week or two before I start a new story so that I can approach it with a clear head. I've had to vary my routine over the years, as I used to write a lot while commuting by train, which is no longer an option. As I have a very demanding day job that pays my bills, I write in the evening after dinner, with headphones on listening to music which thematically matches the story.

MARTIN ROSE (*Bring Me Flesh, I'll Bring Hell*): Routines are best. I like the 1,000 words a day rule, but some days it's a 500 word day, and that's just all there is to it. I used to write on the fly, but what I found is that writing a novel is like driving a car, and sometimes you're so caught up in the scenery, you drive it off the road. Now I make maps. So I'll map out the "scenes" and act accordingly. It's effective, and in some cases, you find interesting detours while still being able to make it to your destination. These days, I begin stories according to moon cycles. I picked up the habit from the Farmer's Almanac, because planting is done by moon cycles, and if you brew wine and mead like me, pitching yeast is also subject to the gravitational pull of the moon. If I write a novel in the time it takes to make champagne, there's few better ways to celebrate the creative process.

PEGGY A. WHEELER (*Chaco*): I'm generally a pantser. I may or may not create a high-level outline before putting my fingers on the keyboard, but nothing too detailed. I generally start with a title, the character cast, an idea of how I want the story to end, and I just dig in and do it. I don't have a specific ritual (no lighting candles, or listening to specific music, or chanting to the gods before I sit down to my laptop). I dedicate between two and four hours a day to writing or writing-related activities, but not on a specified schedule. The exception is if I'm on a roll—if I'm in the zone and busting through writing a book, I've been known to write for thirteen hours without a break, or I may get up at two or three a.m. because something has come to me that I must write, or I'll forget. Otherwise, I put my butt in a chair, and my fingers on the keyboard, some time every day.

TODD KEISLING (*The Smile Factory*): I usually don't start writing until I have a tentative title for the piece, an idea of where to start, and a place where the story will end. Those factors can change over the course of the story, but I prefer to have something in place before I begin.

LORI R. LOPEZ (*The Strange Tale of Oddzilla*): I'm not a fast writer. I can spend hours on one paragraph. One line. I edit as I work, and I care about the wording. I check for redundancy. And I think. A lot. It's a slow process. Yet it works for me. The times I've written a few pages in a burst, I spent days checking them for redundancy, languishing. This is what works in my case. And as much time as I devote to the lines, caring about their balance and flow, their precise wording, I still might polish a sentence further once the story is told. (My poems are stories, too, by the way. I'm a storyteller.) An average day could yield 500 to 1,000 words of serious fiction. A good day 2,000, though humor comes easier. It isn't about how many words I put together in a day. It's about choosing the right words.

PAUL FLEWITT (*Poor Jeffrey*): Well, first I sacrifice several virgin goats and draw their blood into the pen, consorting with a whole host of demons... Did you know that if you give a roomful of demon monkeys a pen, they will produce the written works of Dennis Wheatley in a year?

Honestly, I don't really have a set process or ritual that I go through. I just sit with a pen and a pad of paper and write. I probably write for a couple of hours each day, sometimes a little more, sometimes a little less. I don't put pressure on myself to be writing all the time; if I'm not feeling it one day, I don't write. It's really that simple. There's no set word or page count that I try to hit every day. I find that targets don't help me; they hinder. So, I write until I'm tired and if that turns out to be half a page, a page, or several pages, I see any progress as good progress. I always make sure to not write at all on weekends. That is much needed family time, and a time to recharge my batteries. The only time I'll write on weekends is if I have a story nearing completion. That's probably the only strict rule that I stick to.

GIL VALLE (*A Gathering of Evil*): My process is fairly simple. I craft a story in my head and how I want it to end. Then I write a very brief outline of how I am going to get from beginning to end. Once I have that, I just pound away at the keyboard. For the most part, I stick to the outline, but I sometimes come up with a new idea while I am writing the manuscript, and I just wing it and go with it. If the new idea affects something earlier in the book, I go back and work on it right away. Grammar and typos aside, I keep the story itself up to date before I continue.

Once I have my ideas and my outline, it doesn't take me long to finish a book. I typically have a first draft complete in less than three months. I write at home using my laptop, and most of my writing is done on weekends since I work a full-time 9-to-5 job. It all just comes together quickly for me, and I am able to visualize every scene in my mind, and I do my best to focus on every little detail and bang it all out. The little details are what make a story complete. I try to put myself in every character's shoes, and, if you are familiar with my work, the story is often told from different perspectives (perpetrators, victims, family members, etc.). I really try to get into my characters and everything about their emotions, their desires, and their fears.

JESSICA MCHUGH (*Rabbits in the Garden*): I'm one of those luddites who still uses paper and pen. I've drafted twenty-six books and over a hundred short stories by hand first, then dealt with the editing/rewriting process either on the computer or by printing it out and editing by hand in a binder. The latter process is a lot more time-consuming, but it feels more natural. Because I work on multiple projects at once, I don't aim to hit a daily word count or even follow a specific routine, because I could be working on the story with the nearest deadline but get stuck and have to change my scenery and/or the piece in order to soldier on. I follow emotion and inspirado so it doesn't feel like I'm trying to squeeze blood out of a stone if something's not flowing right.

SCOTT M. BAKER (*Nazi Ghouls from Space*): When I begin a project, I spend a few weeks plotting out the story on 3x5 cards, one card per chapter. I use them because it's easier to jot down notes (dialogue, character points, descriptions) and re-arrange the scenes as needed. My usual writing time is at night after the rest of the family has gone to bed and I have no disturbances (except for the cats who share my study). I set myself a goal of 10,000 words a week, which is reasonable. That way, I can have the first draft completed within three months. Once the first draft is completed, I set it aside for a month while I research my next project, and to give my beta readers time to review the manuscript, then I go back and edit.

J. STEFFY (*Evolution of a Monster*): I write whenever I have free time after the rest of the family is asleep. In a recliner, quietly.

S.A. COSBY (*My Darkest Prayer*): If I'm working on a full-length novel or novella, I like to write a detailed synopsis of where I think the story will go. Once I have that, I come up with a title. Then I write everyday I can until the first draft is finished.

J.C. MICHAEL (*Pandemonium*): I couldn't be a writer who writes in short bursts, or who works to a pattern of a set number of words per day. I like to let my thoughts flow and the writing to flow from them, so it suits me to write, and write, and write, until I have to stop. This isn't too much of a problem because I don't write on a regular basis. I can go for weeks writing nothing other than jotting down the odd idea, and even, then most ideas just rattle around in my head. Then, once I actually seem to have a story that is ready to be born, I can sit down and write for hours on end. It can play havoc with my spelling and grammar, as I think far faster than I can type, but that's what editing's for.

CHAD LUTZKE (*The Same Deep Water as You*): I have no set time of day I write, but I try and do it every day or it turns into a hiatus that could potentially last weeks. I'm all for letting the inspiration lead you, but I'm also one for discipline. If you're just sitting around waiting for the story to write itself, you're wasting a lot of time. Sometimes there's a hill to climb before you can coast.

EDWARD LEE (*White Trash Gothic*): Every five or ten years, it seems, I change my work environment. Right now I write outside on a screened porch in Florida. Fresh air and chirping birds! I admit I'm an oddball. Last night it was forty-nine degrees and I was sitting out here working in multiple jackets; in the summer, it's the opposite: ninety degrees, high humidity, and my dumb ass is writing outside with a cheapo fan blowing. Now that I'm nearly social security age, I've found that I've lost a lot of creative energy. For over twenty years, I'd write a thousand words a day at least, every day, but now it's half that or a little less, but I still manage to get some work done.

RHONDA PARRISH (*Fae*): Every book, every project, is different. Routine would be lovely, but I kind of suck at routine. In theory, when I'm on deadline I write a certain number of words every workday, first thing, before I even check e-mail. I say in theory because some days it works better than others, but I'm striving for consistency. Because routine is the thing that will get my butt in the chair to write that first draft. Also, because the first draft is the hardest stage for me, I try to get it over with as quickly as possible—like pulling off a Band-Aid. I write it as fast as I possibly can and work very hard to keep myself from revising. Because as soon as I stop writing to revise, that's when everything stalls out. That is, at least, when it comes to fiction. nonfiction is a whole other creature. But like I said, every book is different in its own way.

RICHARD GODWIN (*Savage Highway*): I write anywhere that is quiet. And that has a desk.

BARBARA ELLE (*Death in Vermillion*): I consider writing my work, though I also work full-time. I like to get into a "writing head" by planning the time and pla7 76bnjjnh yce for writing sessions. I like to sit down at my kitchen table with my notes, including a very structured plot outline and a running list of ideas, dialogue snippets, and edits. When inspiration strikes, I like to make notes on my iPhone, or scribble on scraps of paper. I incorporate these notes into to this running list, which I print out to help focus on a particular scene. I understand some writers are pantsers; I'm more of a planner.

Yet, it always comes down to sitting at my laptop, opening the Word document and letting the words flow from my fingers to the page.

STEPHEN SPIGNESI (*Dialogues*): I usually write every day from 7 a.m.-ish to 1 p.m., but sometimes that time is spent doing research instead of actually writing, particularly when working on a nonfiction book.

I don't use a laptop, so I'm always at my desk. I work in total silence, unless the project requires otherwise. For example, I am currently working on a book about Elton John, so, of course, I am revisiting all his songs and albums in order to be able to write about them. But usually, I prefer no background sounds whatsoever.

GREG HICKEY (*The Friar's Lantern*): I wrote the initial draft of my first novel in 2008 and 2009, during the year after I graduated from college. I was living overseas in Sundsvall, Sweden and Cape Town, South Africa, and coaching and playing for local baseball teams. My baseball responsibilities were limited to a few practices each week and games on weekends. In Cape Town, I also had a temporary day job for two or three months. So I had a lot of spare time to devote to writing.

When I returned to the U.S. in April 2009, I got a part-time job and enrolled in graduate school. In 2011, I accepted a full-time job as a forensic scientist, a position I still hold today. With less available free time, my current approach is to handwrite during lunch breaks at work and type up what I've written at the end of each week. This schedule allows me to write about 2,000 words per week, which adds up to a draft of a good-sized book at the end of a year. As long as I put in thirty to sixty minutes a day and write 2,000-plus words a week, I end up making decent long-term progress.

M. NAIDOO (*Where Sleeping Lies Lie*): Since I am far from being able to quit my day job, I have to use every spare minute to write, which pretty much restricts me to evenings, late nights, and weekends. Trying to turn out a certain word count per session doesn't work for me since I'd end up worrying about numbers more than about content. I have days when the words just flow, and I can't stop writing. On others, it's like banging my head against the wall hoping for words to fall out of my ears. I found that over time they do even each other out, so I stopped getting worked up when the cursor refuses to move. It's all part of the process, and I learned to trust it.

BEN OHMART (*The Rerun of Dracula*): I don't do as much writing as I used to because I find that the people who are really successful at their writing only do that one thing. They pour their time into it, and therefore their soul, like a Stephen King or Woody Allen. I spend much of my time publishing the works of others.

And success begets success. When someone wants it, it's easier to keep producing it. King has what he's called "a marketable obsession," and I don't. I like comedy, which is important—it's important to laugh—but it's not important to awards and not everyone laughs at the same thing, and so, though I had some success, I didn't find enough to have me steal time away from publishing books, which brings in money.

But when I did write, I could do ten pages at a time—and we're talking scripts, radio, or screenplay pages—easily. I can flip it on and off like a switch, and I've never had writer's block. I usually don't plot things; I just have an idea of what I want to do and keep going with what I think is funny. If it doesn't make me smile, I hold the backspace button down until I'm at the last laugh line and go again. I keep going until I get to ten pages, or more, if the end is in sight.

B.R. STATEHAM (*Murder Is Our Business*): Some writers sit down and outline every character, every chapter, ever node of information into minute detail before they take up writing. I don't. Again, that first 'image' comes to mind. It's like the old Alfred Hitchcock's 'McGuffin.' The McGuffin is the essence which creates, or sums up, the whole story. I have to capture the reader in the first chapter. If I do, from there on I continue to write traps, red herrings, dead end alleys, anything which will keep the reader from leaving. I'm not saying I'm good at it. I'm just saying that's what I try to do.

DOUGLAS BRODE (*Sweet Prince: The Passion of Hamlet*): Writing is a commitment. If you get up with plans to write, but over coffee think to yourself, ah, it's beautiful out, I'll go for a walk and write on a day when it rains, then you will always be a "would-be" writer, never a real writer. For me (and note that I'm now seventy-five and no longer have to earn a living for me and my family as a teacher), I love to sleep late. When I do begin to wake, I think over—while totally fresh—the chapter I'm going to write today. During those early minutes, things take shape (for me at least) beautifully. Then I get up, kiss my wife, play with our pups, have a cup of coffee and a bagel, catch a few minutes of the news on TV, and then off I go to my office.

I quickly read over the previous chapter that I wrote the day before, maybe make a few changes here and there, then it's off and running on the next chapter. Some days it flows, others it doesn't. No matter—get that chapter written without pausing to get depressed about it, no matter how horrible you fear it might turn out. Probably won't be that bad when you look it over again. After two or so hours of this, I'm free to do whatever I want. Then, in the evening, after watching a movie or late night talk shows, I head back to the office and go over what I wrote. Maybe improve it a little. Think it through and what will logically follow in the next chapter. I go to sleep thinking about that, wake in the morning, and so it goes…day after day…maybe I produce something worthwhile from all this. Maybe not. That's for others to decide when they read it. All I know is that I gave it everything that I had to give. Or, as a playwright named Murray Schisgal told me when I was young: "Don't worry about whether it's good or bad. That's for others to say, and none of them know anything anyway. Some will say it's bad, others that it's good. All you have to be able to say is: 'good or bad, it's mine! I wrote that. And talked someone into publishing it.'" Think of Sinatra—"I did it my way." Because good or bad, no one can ever take that away from you.

Editing and Rewriting   3

STEWART O'NAN (*Snow Angels*): This is what writing is: having the patience to change what you've written until it's exactly what you mean to say.

MICHELLE BOWSER (*A Gross Miscellany*): I edit on days I have trouble finding the muse, and then when I'm done with the writing and have no choice. I treat it the same way I do the writing—I work on it every day until it's done.

At the end, I always hire a copy editor and then have a fight with them about their story line critiques I didn't ask for, but copy editors *are a must*! They will find the typos and continuity errors that I don't see because I know what it's supposed to say, and my brain automatically fills it in when I reread it. I've noticed a surge in simple, obvious mistakes in books lately because authors didn't bother to hire an editor. Even with one, there can still be errors, but without them it's alphabet carnage.

A note about copy editors: as much as I value them, I'd like to put them all in the Thunderdome until they can agree on stuff. I've worked with many different ones and they all have different ideas about what is and isn't acceptable.

ANDY RAUSCH (*Bloody Sheets*): One thing that helps me tremendously that I never hear anyone talking about is reading the work out loud. Nothing helps me locate an out of place word or phrase like reading the piece out loud. When you do that, you find the rhythm and cadence of the piece, and sometimes there will be a clunky word or two.

MARK SLADE (*A Six Gun & the Queen of Light*): I don't always re-edit unless something doesn't seem right. But that usually happens while I'm working on the story, not later.

GARY VINCENT (*Darkened Hills*): I am a very fast writer, and with speed comes *a lot* of typos. My personal rule is to get the idea out on paper first and then go back to correct. I don't think I'm ever totally happy with the number of rounds of proofing that I do, and even with the help of other copy editors, I am always finding things after the fact. (Usually after the book is in print.) Still, it never really hurts to at least attempt to do the best job you can.

BECKY NARRON (short-story writer, numerous anthologies): I let someone read my story, and then I go back with their suggestions and rework it as many times as it needs to be done. My rough drafts are really rough. As far as editing, I get it as clean as I can and then my poor editor gets to try to clean up. Bless his heart. He makes me look much better and smarter than I really am. I never try to edit my own stories. Other people's writing I can, but I tend to be blind when it comes to my own. I guess because I've looked at it for so long.

JOE R. LANSDALE (*Bubba Ho-Tep*): I mostly edit as I go. I read what I wrote the day before, correct, and move on. I try and average no less than three to five pages a day, and frequently, I get more. That way, I've done most of the heavy lifting as I go. I get halfway, and then I start over and edit and then continue, as this gives me momentum, then give it a light polish. If editors or proof readers come up with good suggestions, I listen. If not, I ignore them.

CHRIS ROY (*Her Name Is Mercie*): I start with an idea and expand on it. Add a little here, omit a little from there. It builds and is revised constantly, and the final product is something people will read and go, "Wow! How the hell…," and will never know how much work went into it.

GRAHAM MASTERSON (*The Manitou*): I start every morning by reading through what I wrote the day before, correcting it if necessary. That means that when I have finished a book, it is more or less completely edited, and I can simply press send, and it's gone. I print out one copy which I auction online and send the proceeds to an orphanage in Strzelin, in southern Poland, which I support. For me, one of the essences of good fiction writing is to make readers feel that they are actually living the story rather than reading about it. This is a technique that I used to discuss for hours with my friend William S. Burroughs. He called it being "El Hombre Invisible"—the invisible man. Using simple but accurate language and almost musical rhythms, you can involve readers and not make them feel that you are lecturing them or showing off your research, and you don't break the spell by using a word that they won't immediately understand.

ELKA RAY (*Saigon Dark*): I often compare writing to wood-working. The more times you sand something, the smoother it gets. If you're not frustrated, bored, and exhausted by your manuscript, it's unfinished.

EDDIE GENEROUS (*Radio Run*): I like to write something and then leave it alone for a month, rewrite and leave it for another month. After the third rewrite, I usually sub it. That's with the long stuff. With short stories, I write and rewrite and polish all within a couple weeks, sometimes a couple days if I'm really feeling a story.

I know lots of people would use beta readers, and I probably would too if I knew some people better and trusted their opinions. I did have a beta reader once, and it was helpful, but I'm breakneck. I need the shit done, and I don't like filling my plate with owed favors. When you run a magazine and a press, you see people doing you a favor, and a day later they've popped a manuscript into your mailbox, so that shit can get sticky.

BRIAN BARR (*Dark Ripple: When Lovecraft Met Crowley*): I go over my stories a few times to catch what I can, then I hire a friend to do the edits. Sometimes I'll take out passages, or add them, if I think a story is too short or long. Sometimes I'll simplify the language, or make it more prosey, depending on the type of story it is.

JOHN W. WOOD (*White Crow*): I do it all wrong, apparently, because I edit as I write. I have an editor who has been my friend for years. He has a beautiful mind, and we work well together. I send him several chapters at a time to edit while I continue the story. He will call me and say, "You need more wagons or carts, and your character can't carry that many hides to market." Or "I checked, the cavalry units carried more ammunition than that, you need to change it." Or the one that grinds me, "Why did you put that in there? It has nothing to do with the story!" I thought it was pretty cool, but of course, he's right, and it's taken out, but I save the idea, because it might work in another story. So I guess I can say that I really enjoy the editing process as we do it.

G. MIKI HAYDEN (*Strings*): I write clean, and I don't rewrite much. I simply have written for so many years. I strive for polish, which is how I actually entered into teaching and line editing as a trade. I have two writing instructionals in print, by the way: a style guide with all you will ever really need as to grammar, punctuation, and a-rose-between-your-teeth style—*The Naked Writer* published as an ebook by Curiosity Quills—and *Writing the Mystery*, now in its third edition from JP&A Dyson.

JENNIFER BROWN (*Hate List*): I am a strong believer in revisions. And I am a strong believer in people having the jobs they have for a reason. What I mean by this is, I don't fight them. I figure my editor is the one person in this world who wants my book to succeed as much as I do, and I figure she has knowledge about books and publishing that I don't have, because I'm not an editor (just as I have knowledge about them that she doesn't have, because she's not an author), so I really try to go with her suggestions. Not always, of course, but most of the time. I trust in the process, even if it means I have to cut huge portions of my manuscript—sometimes even multiple chapters—and write new scenes entirely. Ideas are infinite, and to think I've landed on *the only* correct ideas and *the only* true arrangement of words to convey those ideas would be a terrible mistake.

Generally, my manuscripts go through two rounds of my own edits, then a round from my agent, then at least two—sometimes three—developmental and line edits from my editor, then a couple copyedits, then one last round of proofreading before it goes to print.

DAVID CLARK (*Game Master*): My first draft is pretty much just a rough draft straight through from start to finish with minimum focus on grammar and spelling. Once that draft is done, I go through it, fixing spelling and grammar. The next pass through, I try to read it like a reader and add description and content where I believe more is needed to set the scene or remove if I think it is overdone. Less is definitely more when it comes to that. Fourth pass, I use various different pieces of software to identify and remove any adverbs, passive tense, or weak words. For the final pass, I let Microsoft word read it back to me as I listen. This is useful for pacing, tempo, and smoothness. Only when I'm through each of these passes do I open the door and let someone else, beta reader or editor, read it.

SAMANTHA BRYANT (*Face the Change: Menopausal Superheroes*): Because I've always been a pantser—or as I like to call it, to make it sound more dignified: a discovery process writer—my first drafts take a long time. I rewrite while I'm still drafting, so I work in loops where I move forward until I make a change that affects earlier material, then I go back and fill that in or rewrite the relevant sections until I move forward again.

I work with a couple of critique partner and groups, too, and exchange work while it's still in process. That idea horrifies some of my writer-friends, but I find that I appreciate getting reaction while things are still soft and not so solidified in my mind. You have to know yourself and your process to know when to ask for feedback on your work, but I think we all benefit from getting fresh eyes on our work sometime along the way, if only to figure out what didn't actually make it out of your brain and onto the page.

This way of working is slow, I admit. My slowest first draft was four years, and my fastest nine months. But by the time I have a full draft, it's usually not that bad. It can be cleaned up and tweaked rather than being torn apart and reconstructed. I already dissected it and pieced it together over and over again while I was writing that first draft. By the time I get to "the end" for the first time, my Frankenstein monster is pretty close to ready to perform "Puttin' on the Ritz."

CHRIS MILLER (*A Murder of Saints*): Once I start to go back through the manuscript, I start revising and rewriting sections, lines, paragraphs, as well as filling in missing words and fixing typos. I try to catch any grammatical mistakes I can find as well. Often I'll add entire new sections or paragraphs, sometimes entire chapters to fill in more story, and I've also been known to cut paragraphs and even entire chapters when directions change in the story or if it's just fluff. But I actually don't write much fluff anyway, so my manuscripts tend to grow during rewrites. Once through this process, I do it again. It may be twice, it may be five or six times. Depends on the story and how it develops. At some point though, I have to step back and decide it's finished. No manuscript will ever be perfect, and we have to remember that. Perfection is the enemy of done. If we never get it done, we'll never get it published. So once I reach that point,

I send it to an editor/proofreader to give it a run through, then it's on to my agent and publishers.

MAX ALLAN COLLINS (*Road to Peridition*): I don't worry about the first draft much, trying to get something down that I can shape and expand. I do a minium of three full passes, and more when something seems to need more attention.

THOMAS GUNTHER (*The Big Book of Bootleg Horror: Volume Four*): Honestly, I'm not sure I actually have a process. I mean, I learned a lot of stuff in college, but I don't think I really use any of it, at least not consciously. I tend to do a lot of editing while I'm proofing. I never rewrite, though. It's all one big creative movement for me. I never work to change the story a whole lot, which is what I would consider a rewrite. I work to enrich the story, to make it the best it can be. The most important thing for me is clarity and grace, which was pounded into my head by my English professor. Grammar doesn't have to be perfect, it just has to be clear. I don't worry about much more than basic grammar—where all the commas go (and I abuse endashes and emdashes).

JOHN PALISANO (*Night of 1,000 Beasts*): This I usually reserve for times when I have longer free periods. I need to focus and be as distraction-free as possible. Much of my process requires me to read out loud the text. It's something I learned as an actor. It helps me find awkward bits and the cadence of the story. Does it work? I don't know. Reviewers have been all over the map, so I know it works for me personally, and I enjoy it tremendously.

Another big thing I do is to do a quick review of the previous day's work before I dive into new writing, time permitting. Not only does it refresh a mind scattered by daily obligations, but I can often catch typos and other such things as I do so.

MAXWELL BAUMAN (*The Anarchist Kosher Cookbook*): This might sound strange, but I think that editing and rewriting are more fun than the initial writing. It's during the editing phase that I get to know the characters better. I can slow down and see what their world looks like. The story is never perfect the first time through, and that's okay. Once everything is down on paper, I can hit it with a hammer. I read the story out loud to make sure it flows and find any typos, missed words, or redundancies.

BEV VINCENT (*Flight or Fright*): Writing is about a third creation and two-thirds revision, in my experience. It may take me two or three days to write a story in first draft, but I'll then spend the better part of a week—if not more—refining and revising. On the first pass, I typically remove about ten percent of the text. From that point on, I may add or remove, but the first cut, as they say, is the deepest.

I rewrite in two different ways, online and off.

Working with a hardcopy, I'll scribble all over the current draft and key in the changes. When I work this way, I tend to make more sweeping changes—deleting huge swaths of text, writing lengthy additions into the margins, moving paragraphs, often from one page to another.

When I revise a draft on the computer, my focus tends to be more on getting each sentence correct. Finding better words, deleting extraneous words or clauses, searching for repetitions, things like that. Occasionally I may do something more major, like reorder the sentences in a paragraph or shift paragraphs around, but mostly, it's more focused.

I'll alternate between these two types of editing several times during the revision process. I hardly ever keep old drafts, though. If I cut a paragraph, it's gone forever—no record that it ever existed! And if I go back to an old story and revise it before submitting it again, I will typically throw out the previous draft.

PAUL D. BRAZILL (*Cold London Blues*): When I write a novella, I usually write a scene and then go back and tidy it up. Then I do the same thing again and again until I think I've finished. It's usually eighty percent finished when it's done. I sometimes open out scenes a bit more, but I'm very wary of padding out stuff. No domestic drudgery or middle-class soap opera! With short stories, I usually write from start to finish, and it's pretty much done.

TRAVIS WALLACE (*Clues*): Until I do an official edit/rewrite, there is a blurred line. I start everything I do in longhand. I have a journal I carry and if I don't have a journal I use napkins, envelopes, backs of magazines—anything I can get my hands on. I write initial thoughts as far as I can take them and then I wait until I have a next inspired thought and I do it again. When I get enough of these "random" thoughts written, I re-read them to see if there is a pattern. When a pattern is identified, then I start to type each of the longhand sections, adding character depth, descriptors, conversations, scenery, etc. I guess this is my first rewrite, and it is to give depth. I also edit any low-hanging fruit at this point.

The next rewrite happens when I start putting these random typed thoughts in whatever chronology the book will follow, and during this, I add connectors and transitions. Usually I give more voice (I start drinking) to the scene. I tend to type the whole thing from scratch again rather than making edits on my manuscript.

My next edit/rewrite doesn't occur until I am close to 60,000 to 80,000 words. I put everything to the side for a few weeks and then read it like a new book, only using a red pen to edit and identify as many holes as I can. I go in, make the changes, and if I am satisfied with what I have, I try to find someone to read it and give me their feedback before I do another edit and try to submit for publication.

All this said, I have only been through this entire process one time. I am working on two more pieces now and at the second/third stage of my edit/rewrite process. For me, stage two and three happen simultaneously. If I don't throw them away soon, I will get more structured so I can get them submitted.

PAUL HEATLEY (*An Eye for an Eye*): Editing is where you realize everything you've done wrong. It's where you come to the crushing conclusion that if you want to save this work, you might have to rewrite the whole thing from scratch. You might even have to give it up. Both of these things have happened to me a few times now, and it's devastating. Still, editing is also where you get to fix problems and polish things up. I'm a diligent editor, always have been. I read a work over and over and over again, trying to make sure it's right. My book *Fatboy* was saved by an edit and rewrite. If I hadn't put the time in on it, it could be sitting languishing in a file somewhere. Editing is integral, and it's where you find yourself as a writer.

BRIAN JAMES LANE (*Fright Feast*): Editing is the necessary drudgery of writing. I have a hard time not completely rewriting when editing because it's simply more fun. But when I know I must produce something as I have reworked it to death, I do have a method which helps to keep me on task.

I use Microsoft Word to write. I have installed a plugin which reads the text and highlights words as it goes. If I just read it in my head, I can miss a mistake a thousand times. If I hear it aloud, I can catch it more easily.

I like working on dual monitors. It helps to have the rough draft in the left screen and the document you are revising on the right. You have the plugin read the text and highlight each word as it goes on the left and then edit simultaneously on the other screen. It's like watching paint dry, but it keeps my mind from wandering. You can do this on one screen, too. Simply have both documents open and sized to half the screen. It may get somewhat claustrophobic, but I have done it successfully this way, too.

I have others read the draft when possible, as well. Non-writers, though, may miss the mark on all but mechanics. Fellow writers are a little better. The best are professional editors. Bless them for their job! This is a luxury, however. If a publisher is paying for that service, then I don't mind. If it's on my dime, I would rather self-edit. I'm kind of a tightwad that way. Be careful, however, as the adage rings true—you get what you pay for.

CARMEN AMATO (*Cliff Diver*): I learned how to write and edit while working for the CIA where you write for policymakers who expect to see the bottom line in the first sentence. Your prose has to be articulate and impactful, in specific formats for specific publications, and there are tight deadlines. I apply the same discipline to my fiction.

PAUL TREMBLAY (*Head Full of Ghosts*): Every writer is different. But I do a lot of editing as I go. I start each day by editing what I wrote previously. If I'm working on a novel, I typically edit the chapter I'm in before adding to it. By the time I'm done with a full draft, I've already edited it quite a bit. For the final edits, I print out the manuscript and usually read it out loud. Reading out loud helps me catch typos and allows me to hear if the desired rhythm to the sentences is off.

LILY LAMB (*The Dowling House*): I read and rewrite, listen to it out loud and then rewrite again. I keep doing this until I'm satisfied. I also have my husband read it over to check my grammar. English is my second language, so I need him to check my punctuation, syntax, etc. I didn't study English formally so I have a lot of syntax issues, plus I tend to sprinkle commas like I sprinkle salt over every dish.

CHARLES LYNNE (*What Screams In the Dark*): My editing skills are very lacking. I have ADD and ADHD, so when I write, my hands can't keep up. Lots of misspellings and wrong words. I heavily rely on my sister, who is an editor, to help me.

MIKE PURFIELD (*In a Blackened Sky Where Dreams Collide*): I don't rewrite in the traditional sense. During the writing process, I might cycle back and add or adjust. My brain concentrates on a book for three to four months (the time it takes to write it), so I should have all my bases covered. If not, oh well. Maybe if I didn't notice, the reader won't notice.

The second time I look at the draft, I spend my time fixing grammar and cutting. Sometimes I'm repetitious or wordy in a draft. I rarely fix story or plot or anything major. All those issues are once and done in the first draft.

I don't edit by committee unless an editor is interested in buying a short story (this happens rarely). Sometimes I go to a writing group and share my pages and get feedback. I like to hear their responses. No disrespect to what they have to say, but I don't take most of what they say too seriously. One perspective does not make a break or story. Just like one editor or one reader doesn't make or break a story.

Editing for grammar makes perfect sense. You want something to be readable. Editing for marketability is insane and has no place in art. A majority of writers do this, and that's their business and dream. They want to take their voice and vision and rewrite it until it fits a publishing house or a salable niche in hopes they will sell more of his/her small cut.

Editing to discover. Maybe people do so many drafts because they have no voice and they don't know what their book is about. To this, why the hell are you writing a novel? Stop the madness. Stop wasting your time with such a big task. Writing shouldn't be a chore. When you're sitting at the keyboard, time should be flying by. Characters should be taking over and action should be flowing. It should be fun. You should be making people feel. You should have something to say and not be afraid to say it. When you are fearless, then you don't need to do so many drafts because you wrote down what you had to say.

ISOBEL BLACKTHORN (*Clarissa's Warning*): I tend to avoid doing much editing until I have a whole first draft. That draft might only be 50,000 words, or even less. Once I have it, I set it aside for a few weeks. Then I sit down in my armchair and edit with a pen. I craft sentences, fix grammar, improve the quality of the writing, the word choices, and so on. I add in paragraphs when things need fleshing out. I stylize the dialogue. The tedious part is punching all that into the document on the computer. I find that a chore. I print out another version and repeat the process. I would call that my second draft. After that, I send out to beta readers and have a good long break and then come back to it. I prefer reading hard copy, but I have recently taken to editing onscreen, which is really proofreading to get the story from second to final draft. For me, the best part of writing is those stages between first and second draft when the story grows and the themes emerge.

BOB VAN LAERHOVEN (*Return to Hiroshima*): Usually, I have rewritten every novel I've published about three times. The last rewriting was always done by hand. Editing and rewriting by hand is a FPITA (fucking pain in the ass, sorry, excuse, pardon), but it works: automatically, you slow down, and when you slow down, you think clearer.

Furthermore, I am a great believer in gruesome cruel editing—kill your darlings!—by professional third parties. Leo De Haes, my editor with my publishing house Houtekiet Uitgevers, seemed to draw sadistic satisfaction from mutilating my manuscripts with a large hatchet. But the result, oh miracle, was that they were better afterwards.

HEYWOOD GOULD (*Fort Apache, The Bronx*): I rewrite constantly. I agonize over the smallest issue even though I know the reader doesn't really demand perfection and is a lot more forgiving of my work than I am.

DAVID L. TAMARIN (*BOLO: Sociopaths on a Rampage*): It's typical to spend much more time rewriting than writing. Writing is getting your ideas out, and rewriting them is re-working what you wrote so that it sounds better and has no errors. I don't correct for grammar or spelling, I just write when it's a first draft. If I need to do research, then I save that for later drafts. The story comes alive slowly, sometimes through different drafts. This is most true with a screenplay. I did about a dozen drafts on my last screenplay, a true-crime story based on the real New York "Cannibal Cop." With a short story, I get most of it right on the first draft but always need to rewrite it at least once.

BRET MCCORMICK (*Headhunters from Outer Space*): I tell the story as quickly as possible. When a draft is ready to read, I go through it slowly, inserting additional information and paying particular attention to any questions I think may arise in the reader's mind. In most cases, I address these as thoroughly as possible, unless the mood of the piece requires a bit of uncertainty on the part of the reader. I like the work of Elmore Leonard, and I value his advice to aspiring writers, namely go ahead and cut out all the stuff that readers are going to skip over anyway. This usually means leaning heavily on dialogue and keeping the descriptions trim and compelling. Clever turns of phrase can easily take a reader out of the story, so you need to be clever but sneaky about it. Vonnegut's a good example of a writer who's all about the clever, consequently the reader is never totally immersed in the story. The story is subordinate to his cleverness. Not that I'm complaining. I like Vonnegut. He was one of my favorite writers when I was a young man. Now days, I'm more inclined to be more impressed with someone like Jim Harrison. There's plenty of cleverness in his books, but he presents it in such an offhand way that you rarely depart from the reality he's created. The great thing about writing is that there's plenty of room for all styles at the literary table.

AUTUMN CHRISTIAN (*Girl Like a Bomb*): Everyone's editing process is different, and you can only find what works for you after you've fumbled through it. But that's the same with everything—the path to enlightenment is built with multiple mistakes.

There is a music inside of the words, and if you listen to it, you can see where each beat needs to go and what the rhythm of the piece should be like. I typically write about five drafts for my novels and two or three for my short stories. It's never been a set process for me, that's just how many it usually takes before I feel it's "good enough."

KURT BELCHER (*Spiders & Stardust*): I've heard "writing is rewriting": just get the idea down first, then worry about making it pretty later. I guess that's true for me, although I generally try to get out as much of it as possible as early as possible. It makes rewriting easier. On rare occasions, big ideas occur to me once I'm done with that part, which require a major rewrite of the material, but I'm usually pretty satisfied with it after a few drafts, requiring only minor edits. The most drafts I've ever done of something I wrote was probably eight or nine, although that was a collaboration with an artist who was pretty involved in building the story.

KASEY PIERCE (*Pieces of Madness*): Every time I work with an editor, I grow that much more as a writer. It takes a very precious attitude to believe that editors are the enemy. Some cat came up to my table once and went on about how editors were "bastardizing the industry" and "shouldn't change someone's work." It was apparent this bastard has never worked with an editor or even in the industry. An unwillingness to learn, and a faux expertise on how it all works, is what makes a creator their own worst enemy. The editor is there to make sure the reader's perception is in line with yours. They're not there to change your too-precious-for-this-world literature.

By the way, I don't claim to have expertise in how it all works either. I think we're all just throwing things at a wall and seeing what sticks. *looks around* I mean, we are all doing that, right?

Rewrites are a pain, but so is the disappointment of a lackluster story. It's time-consuming and while we'd rather be onto the next project, if we don't stop to rework, we'll just have mounds of okay stories. A whole bibliography of half-assed works with unrealized potential. I'd rather have a handful of great stories than a slew of yawns. No one wants to be remembered as "the author that could have been."

DEV JARRETT (*Loveless*): The editing and rewriting process changes every time, for me. I'd like to think I know what the hell I'm doing by now, but the process itself isn't set in stone. I'm always in competition with myself. I want to perform better than I did last time, and that necessitates changes in both the writing and rewriting. The current work in progress had eight different POVs in the first draft, but all the way downstream to today, the fourth draft is combining everything into a single POV. Challenging? Yup. Worth it, not just for the story but also for my own leveling-up? Yup squared.

MELISSA KEIR (*Cowboy, Mine*): Editing is vital. We naturally don't see errors in our own work. We are too close, and our brain puts words and letters in place where they are missing because we know what we wanted to write. Having a friend read through your story isn't enough. While having someone read through your work is a good strategy, it's not enough to become published.

I use a professional paid editor for all my work. She goes through it three times, and that's after I've already done some self-editing. Then a proofer goes through the manuscript as well. After all that, sometimes errors still get through, but I'm much more confident that my work makes sense.

I am a word repeater. One book had an almost blind character and the word I'd used almost a thousand times was "see". My editor always finds a new overused word in my stories. I appear to latch onto a new favorite word for each story.

She's also good for checking if things make sense. I love when I can stump her. Since she lives in California, she hadn't heard of an Alberta Clipper (a cold storm from the Canadian Rockies), so she had to look it up. But that's unusual, mostly I'm thinking what I've written makes sense, but in reality I have hands or other body parts moving independently of a body. Editing just makes sense.

DAVID OWAIN HUGHES (*Brain Damage*): I never edit a project until it's complete. I like to get that first, rough draft down—nail it up quick and dirty, I say, and get it out of your system. Once it's on paper, I like to let it rest for a couple of weeks before going back to draft it. I always allow that sucker to ferment; for the words to take root upon the digital page. I know some authors who edit as they go, but I could never do that.

Also, I draft my work at least three times, which I think is a fair amount. Once I'm happy with it, I get it out to trusted readers and friends who I know will give me honest feedback. Always trust your chosen critics.

JEFF PARSONS (*The Captivating Flames of Madness*): Editing and rewriting is what makes the story worth reading. You want your story to be the best it can be before you hit send on your email. I've only met a handful of writers who can write well in a first draft. That's not me. I start with vague concepts mostly (lot of caveman grunting noises and wild gestures involved). After a long evolutionary path of three to four rewrites, this work turns into something useful, a clear target I can throw rocks at, or in the very least, I'm learning about the many different ways of how to not write a story. Along the way, I get rid of useless wording and make it consistently logical, all of which is about as easy as doing algebra in a foreign language. But it can be done. Your story, when read aloud, should flow seamlessly.

MICHAEL CIESLAK (*Desolation: 21 Tales for Tails*): To paraphrase the Dread Pirate Roberts, editing is the worst. Anyone who tells you different is trying to get you to edit something.

Actually, I spend a lot of time editing other people's material, and that is fairly easy. Editing my own material, however, is something that I will avoid at all costs. I will go out of my way to look for housework rather than edit my own material. I suspect part of this comes from the desire to think that everything came out perfect on the first go. Note to all aspiring writers: It didn't. It absolutely did not come out perfect in the first go.

As for my actual process, the first thing I do when I finish something, barring any looming deadlines, is put it away for a while. After you have spent however long you have been working on something with a project, you are simply too close to see it fairly. You will either ignore obvious flaws and things which need to be changed, or you will decide that the entire thing is awful. The only way to avoid this is through distance and time.

Once the work has lain fallow for a time, I go back to it. The first read through is for content, seeing where the plot lags, where characters act out of character, what scenes can be cut. Note to all aspiring writers: there are always things which can be cut.

I tend to write long. I've gotten better over the years, but I can always count on clear cutting somewhere around 20% of what I have written. I go into the rewrite knowing this, so it doesn't bother me (much) anymore. After this reworking, I start to get down to the nitty gritty, the line edit stuff. Then it's off to the beta readers. Then another round or two of editing and rewriting.

PHIL PRICE (*Unknown*): I hate this part. Once I have completed a manuscript, I go over it a few times, smoothing it out before I send it to the publisher. Lots of authors say that you cannot edit your own stuff, which is correct. How I have managed it in the past is to read each sentence aloud, trying to hear if something is not quite right with structure, etc. It's the unsexy part of being an author.

JESSE DEDMAN (*The Master's Torment*): I have to step away for a bit. Give it some time so that I'm not reading what I think I wrote, but what I actually wrote.

JAMES WATTS (*Them*): I never edit until the story ends. I never use outlines because they stifle the story. And, of course, because life is not outlined. On editing, I will read the manuscript over and over, making notes and changes until I am satisfied that the work is ready to submit.

A.P. SESSLER (*The First Suitor*): On days I'm not writing at the coffee shop, I edit and do rewrites at home. I was told by one successful author never to change anything to appease a publisher because what one hates, another will love, but I've not taken it to heart. I'm still refining myself as a writer and probably will be till the day I die, as writing (skillful use of language) doesn't come to me as naturally as storytelling or lyrics. I won't change the outcome of the story to appease a publisher, but I am fairly flexible on the linguistic aspect.

JASON PARENT (*A Life Removed*): The old axiom is true: a writer is only as good as his or her editors. I surround myself was as many quality folks as I can.

STANLEY B. WEBB (short-story writer, numerous anthologies): I write most of my first drafts in longhand, then leave the stories alone for a long period–weeks, months, sometimes years–before I edit. This delay allows me to read my own prose objectively. I do not hire proofreaders or editors.

Occasionally, I get a new idea for a market with a short deadline, the shortest being about four days. At such times, I edit intensively with only short breaks between revisions. I have placed stories by this process, but I prefer working in the long term.

WADE H. GARRETT (*Pigs: An Extreme Horror Novella*): When I finish a story, it's what I call a rough draft. I then perform a rewrite. This is when I correct errors and flow issues, and even add to the story where it's lacking. I usually add about 10,000 more words in this step. Next, off to my editor. When she is done, off to my proofreaders, which can range from five to 30 people. After I correct any issues my proofreaders find, off to publishing.

RICHARD CHRISTIAN MATHESON (*Scars and Other Distinguishing Marks*): I write every day. I can write anywhere; my office, a diner, a plane. I can write in longhand or a keyboard. I am mostly oblivious to surroundings although annoyed by loud talkers nearby. But I once wrote a short story about that very thing—so even distraction can lead to something.

ANDREW LENNON (*Bound*): I have two processes to my writing, the first, for a longer piece; I go through and plan chapter by chapter. Just a couple of lines worth of notes for each chapter as a guide for myself as I'm going. Granted, I don't always stick to this plan, but it helps to see the desired route, especially if there have been a few weeks between writing one chapter and the next. For short stories, I don't plan at all. I usually have an idea, and then I just sit down and go with it. Quite often, I don't even know the outcome of the story until it's finished because I just follow the route that the tale takes me on. After the story is finished, I go back through it myself, usually making a lot of amendments and tweaks along the way. There's always more to add and even more to cut, and you never notice this the first time around. It's only when doing a re-read that you spot these things.

Once I've done my re-read, I pass it to my wife. She is always completely honest with me and usually has quite a few suggestions and tweaks. I trust her entirely and adjust according to her feedback every time.

After that, I fire it over to the editor. Again, I always feel you should trust your editor. Unless there's a glaring reason not to agree with their amendments or notes, then I go with it. Only if it alters the story in a way I don't like, will I then say that I'm leaving it the way it was originally written. I've always had a good relationship with editors, never had a falling out, so this process obviously works well for both sides.

PEGGY CHRISTIE (*Hell Hath No Fury*): I loathe editing. It's one of those necessary evils, like a colonoscopy. When I finish a story, no matter the length, I put it away. For shorter works, I'll go back in 24-48 hours. If it's something longer, then I'll hide it away for at least a week. Wow, that sounded dirtier than I intended… You have to be able to ignore your first draft for a while, especially if it took a long time to write. I worked on a novel for three years (I got stuck for about a year), and when I finally finished the rough, I put it away for a month. I was so sick of looking at it, there was no way I could start clean-up in an objective manner.

When I start to miss the story, wishing I could work on it again, that's when I'll edit. At that point, I want it to be the best it can be. I never understood folks who think they don't have to do any editing (my mom loved it as is!) or believe editors should do all the work for them. I'm sorry, but that's fucking weak, sloppy, and unprofessional.

I usually do two edits. The first run through is basic housekeeping—grammar, structure, spelling. The second is for character development, looking for plot holes, story progression, fixing inconsistencies, etc. I might run a third time through to see if anything weird catches my eye, like I got a character name wrong or something like that.

Beyond that, it heads into over-editing mode. That's when you get into danger of hacking and slashing all the *good* stuff in your story because you've blinded yourself with all the bad you've deleted or fixed. You start thinking everything you write is awful and why the hell would anyone want to pay money for this? You should be paying them not to read it, and while we're at it, just stop being a writer all together, and go live in a cave because you are just awful.

Then it's time for more booze and coffee. And find yourself a great editor. Even if I were brilliant at editing (which I'm not,) it's still a good idea to get another set of eyes on your work. And I don't mean your mom, dad, spouse, significant other, sibling, or BFF (I made an exception to this rule for my first novel because my BFF was an editor). You need someone who is professional, can be objective, has a death grip on the rules of grammar and language but can work with your idiosyncrasies, and help smooth out the rough patches in your story. If you're really lucky, you can find one that does all that but won't cost the price of a new car.

CHRISTOPH PAUL (*A Confederacy of Hot Dogs*): I like to write three drafts for a novella (and I am a fan of shitty first drafts) with one more draft to line-edit/copyedit and five to six drafts for a novel. I see the first two drafts as a way to discover the character, story, and voice, and the last two to three drafts after that to start cleaning and fixing the book and sentences.

BILLY CHIZMAR (*Widow's Point*): I write stories based off of ideas, or at least that's how it starts. When I go back on the second and third pass, I try to identify what's being loved or what love is lost and then highlight that factor, make it an overarching constant in the story. I didn't realize that until I wrote an essay on my father's writing for an English class, but writing is about love above all else. In any good story, even horror (especially horror), something loved by someone is at stake. I once wrote a story about a haunted beach and didn't realize until the third pass that it was really, on a visceral level, about my little brother and how much I cared about him. When I rewrote the ending with him in mind, the story had the same bones with an entirely different pathos.

JOE X. YOUNG (short-story writer, numerous anthologies): Editing is my Kryptonite; I didn't go to school much. It would be fair to say that I am self-taught in everything, but one of the things I didn't get a handle on was the correct use of grammar and punctuation, which has had a detrimental effect on writing with a view to publication. Partly as a result of this, I always considered writing to be just a release for me and not intended for public consumption. This changed when I was pushed into submitting work as the first short story I sent out was accepted into the Journal of the British Fantasy Society. Since then, I have had the extreme good fortune to have one hundred percent of my submitted work accepted. As far as editing is concerned, I use Grammarly and ProWritingAid to help as far as my understanding of them allows, but for all other aspects, I rely on the good graces of the publishers and their editors to guide my punctuation and grammar. I do the clean-ups as they suggest, and they make me look good.

Rewriting? For submitted short stories, that's a no. I've never rewritten one or been asked to. I have a lot of incomplete stories, some of which are just the basics which need fleshing out, and sometimes something will change which will require a partial rewrite, but it's never extensive; usually a line or two at best.

DEAN M. DRINKEL (*Demonologica Biblica*): The way I write is that I will do perhaps three or four drafts of anything before I really begin the editing process. I love writing the film scripts longhand in notepads. I tend not to edit as I go along, and it's funny sometimes reading back and seeing characters or locations change or even finding obvious plot-holes. Sometimes, if something jumps out whilst I am writing, then I'll write that on the opposite page (as I only write on one page) or in an additional notebook I purchase for each project, which I'll jot down ideas in if and when they come to me. Whenever I start something new I also buy a load of new CDs, as I find that inspirational and (for me anyway) can really drive a project forward. For the scripts, once I've done the first four or so drafts, then I'll do the first typed version in Word and perhaps do another two or three drafts before I am then ready to start the editing process for real.

This will mean printing the document out completely, and then I'll go through it with a number of colored pens, working on the structure, the scenes, the characters, the dialogue, etc. This will enable me to create one final Word version, which I will then print and go through again. When I'm happy that I'm finished with Word, I'll then go to the bespoke script software and retype out the script. Once completed, that will need a print, and I'll be able to ascertain how many pages I am over and then start a mean edit. I'll keep doing this until I am one hundred percent happy. It's a lot of work, but well worth it. I must say though, the editing side of things I don't have a problem doing late at night or early morning before

I work on the other projects. It can be fun, actually. For a completed one hour TV script, it takes me about three or four weeks to complete from start to finish, which isn't too bad (obviously if the money is good, I will speed that up).

For the stories and novellas, I would say that the process is quite similar, but they perhaps take me a little longer as I always seem to be looking for the perfect sentence and can spend a lot of time just staring at the words as I try to figure it all out. I do need to give myself a slap on the wrist sometimes, as I do tend to go over requested word counts, etc., and take some of my stories (the horror ones in particular) to places I'm sure the editors and publishers really wish I wouldn't.

EVANS LIGHT (*Black Door*): Writing is fun. Editing is work.

I constantly have to remind myself not to edit while writing a first draft, not to worry if what I'm writing is good. It's often not. That's what editing is for.

Writing and editing are two very different processes, and not every author is equally skilled at both. Hire the most professional editor you can afford and be open to their feedback.

Time is about the only way to gain enough perspective to successfully edit your own work. Put it away, let it rest. Edit it once you've forgotten what you've written.

If you've completed less than five drafts before finishing a project, there's a high likelihood it could be better with additional editing. Even if you decide to revise a poorly edited project after it's been publicly released, you can never fully bring it back. That inferior product will always be out there, somewhere, to haunt you. Save yourself that misery. Be patient and edit your work fully and properly before releasing it. Future you will thank current you.

MEGAN O'RUSSELL (*Girl of Glass*): When I start a new project, I edit as I go. So every day when I sit down to write, I'll go though and do a first edit on what I wrote the day before. I write all of my projects in three acts. Once I've finished an act, I go through and re-edit that act before sending it on to my secondary reader, then I dive into the next portion. That way, I'm seeing comments on the start of the project as I'm continuing to write.

Once I have all three pieces of the book back, I look at the comments on the project as a whole, then go through and do any rewrites and edits I want. Then I sit down with my loving husband and have him read the whole thing out loud. Yes, he is the most amazing and indulgent person. Hearing the words out loud not only helps me make sure the speech patterns for the characters are consistent, but also slows down my eyes enough to catch a lot of errors I missed before.

After that, I do one more read through before sending the project along to my editors.

ANDREW BUCKLEY (*Hair in All the Wrong Places*): The advice I always offer is that people should finish their first draft. Don't edit as you go, don't go back and rewrite (unless it's unavoidable . . . or you're being threatened with a gun), just keep going until the draft is done. Then go back and do a round of story editing, then a round of line editing. Reread, repeat as many times as necessary, and then release it into the wild.

JOHN BODEN (*Jedi Summer with the Magnetic Kid*): I'm a sloppy writer. I hold no pretense about it. I miss a lot and am usually happy to oblige when things are pointed out from beta readers or editors. I find I get better at seeing mistakes the more I do this. I approach it as an ongoing education of sorts.

LAURA ROBERTS (*Haiku for Lovers*): All writing is rewriting! This is something my professors said when I was in a college-level creative writing program, and it sounds like a cliché, but it's definitely true. You might think you're done with the writing, but as soon as you give the story to a critique group or editor or agent or publisher, someone else will give you their opinion, and then it's right back to work. If you write only for yourself, that's fine, but if you write for publication, the goal is to appeal to a certain audience. The better you know your audience before you begin, the less rewriting you may have to do, but editing is inevitable. I have a love/hate relationship with editing, as I suspect most writers do, because it's often painful, but it's also a learning process where you can grow as a writer. Writing is the fun part, editing is the hard work part, and you need both to get to the finished product. In short, I'm with Dorothy Parker when it comes to editing: "I hate writing; I love having written."

ERIN SWEET AL-MEHAIRI (*Breathe, Breathe*): I put more focus into editing than writing, as I believe in not editing much as you write, but later. I will, and often do, set aside a piece and come back to it months later to revise. I'd be too close to it otherwise. I ask for help from some trusted readers on content, especially on poems or short flash pieces or stories. I always believe in hiring a very good content and copy editor and a separate proofreader no matter how you publish (even if submitting to publisher). I often rewrite many sentences just to get a perfect lyrical prose tone I want. I always read my things out loud to find errors or flow hiccups. I've tried to read from a mountain top in Barcelona, but no one was listening (not really).

H.R. BOLDWOOD (*The Corpse Whisperer*): I edit a great deal as I go, keeping a close eye on developmental issues, like pacing, character motivation and plot logic to help prevent major rewrites. This flies in the face of a lot of the advice out there, but I've found that scrutinizing my work early on makes for fewer edits at the back end. That said, if I have a brainstorm and see a scene unfolding out of sequence, I will stop and write it while it's fresh. After I've run through the work a couple of times, I pass it along to a crew of beta readers for their thoughts, comments, and suggested edits.

JULIA BRAMER (*The Vitamin D Treatment*): Editing and rewriting are like getting showered and dressed to start your day. You might wake up inherently fabulous, but you will soon stink and reveal the sleep in your eyes, the sour breath, and the mussed up hair the second anyone takes a good hard look at you. Revisions make your work clean, readable, and understandable. Anything less is lazy and offensive.

RANDEE DAWN (*Home for the Holidays*): Editing is a necessary evil. I spent far too much of my early writing years believing my first drafts were final drafts, and not understanding that what's in my head might not be what people were reading on the page. I am absolutely not a fan of either editing or rewriting, but following a critique or required changes by editors, I will do both. And sometimes—okay, most of the time—what emerges is a much better story. That's what keeps me sane during the revising period.

LANNY LARCINESE (*I Detest All My Sins*): I don't always play well with others. My compliance with editors is in direct proportion to confidence that they understand my story, themes, and voice. I don't lose sight of genre conventions. I write crime, yet different from mere "mystery" or "thriller." With every editorial suggestion, I try to balance the story I want to tell with the story that will sell. Though I may not take some advice literally, I search out the underlying principle of what they're telling me; e.g. what to me is interesting insight into character, to an editor unduly slows the action. So maybe I won't eliminate the passage or scene as suggested, but might cut it down. I always self-edit previous work before adding new material.

KATE JONEZ (*Lady Bits*): Nothing is more beautiful than a second draft that's had a little rest. All the missteps become clear. Polishing is much more rewarding than grinding out a first draft.

SCOTT M. GORISCAK (*Horrorism*): Always be open-minded to discussion. No one is perfect. We all think in different paradigms. Listen to your editor's ideas; they might just point out something in the story you didn't see when you wrote it, especially if you are a late-night writer like myself. Never hurts to have an additional set of eyes on your work.

ADRIENNE DELWO (*Hero Academy*): Writing is all about creativity. For editing, you have to take a step back and think analytically and critically. Each scene, each paragraph, each sentence, and finally, each word has to be important or it doesn't belong. What extra words or ideas are cluttering up your story? What can be pared down or combined to make it more efficient, eloquent, or powerful? Be ruthless and cut what needs to be cut, even if you love it.

ESSELL PRATT (*Sharkantula*): When writing, my approach is to go in with a broad idea of how the story will progress from start to finish. This gives me the direction I need to take towards completion. However, I allow myself to meander and take alternate routes as the story desires. Once complete, I'll let it simmer for a short time and then begin my edits from the beginning towards the end. I don't actually make the changes, but instead track the changes and add comments into the document, much like the editor of a press would. Then I let it sit once again. The third pass is where the changes and rewrites take place, allowing time to wrap my head around the final product and ensure it is the best I can make it. I will repeat the steps if needed.

GEORGE LEA (*Strange Playgrounds*): Editing and rewriting are the most difficult parts of the process. In that interest, I do a fair bit of freelance editing work for individuals, small presses, academics etc, as this helps me to hone those instruments. This is often difficult with your own work, but it's the most essential part of the process; where the unrefined lump of inspiration becomes something clear and crystallised.

Distance is a very positive thing; after I've finished a first draft, I will often put the story away for a long, long time, so that I sometimes forget having written it. This helps to establish some degree of critical distance for when I come back to it, allowing me to assess it as a reader might.

Even then, it's difficult to have anything like an objective eye, which is why I find it useful to have a number of readers around me who will give me honest, critical feedback. This particularly helps me to establish whether or not a piece works at base level or if it's simply too abstruse, vague, personal etc.

ERIC J. GUIGNARD (*That Which Grows Wild*): Editing and revising are part of the writing cycle. No one shines by publishing the first draft of what they write. I revise as I write, although most people would argue just to write first and then, once complete, go back and revise, but I've developed my own process. But regardless of when you do it, treat editing and revising as enjoyable necessities of writing. Each time you go back into it, you're making your work cleaner, stronger, better. Additionally, I compose on a word processor, but when I'm done and want to do a final read-through/edit, I change the font style and font size, and print everything, and then edit the old-fashioned way, with a red pen. You'll find errors every time that you overlooked on-screen.

MERCEDES M. YARDLEY (*Pretty Little Dead Girls*): It's quite easy to polish a piece of work so thoroughly that it becomes ground down. Whatever raw, beautiful gem that you originally had there can be crushed into dust. There's a point where you have to let it go. I'll open a piece, reread the last section I wrote, and edit that. Then I'll write something new and put it away. Next time I open that document, I'll edit what I had just written, and so on. When I'm finished, I'll print the entire thing out and go through it with a pen. I time this for a family trip so I read the novel aloud to my husband while we drive. It helps me catch things that I miss on the computer screen. The second set of ears is helpful, too, because he often picks up on things I've missed. I've seen the story so many times by then that I know it all by heart, and will often assume the reader knows the situation as well as I do. Then I send it to my agent, who sends it back with more edits.

ROBERT FORD (*The God Beneath My Garden*): Every writer has their own approach on editing and rewriting, but when I write, I tend to write a bit slower to make it tighter and cleaner on my first draft. There will always be certain things that slip through in the heat of the moment, but overall, I write fairly clean. I look at the first draft as a lump of clay I'm sculpting, and often I'll go back and detail it, putting in expansions on details or filling in some back story here and there.

C. HOPE CLARK (*Murder on Edisto*): I firmly believe you cannot edit too much, and rewriting produces miracles. I have no trouble with throwing away a chapter, a character, or a climax that isn't working, and I have easily tossed them all in some story in the past. My first novel was trashed twice, the full novel, keeping only the outline and starting over. I didn't find any sign of voice until I did. Frankly, by the time I've written a 90,000-word novel, I've thrown away at least that many words.

Editing is the most fun part of writing, in my opinion. The first draft is like running through mud; like I said, I'm slow with it. But the editing is exciting. A chance to add depth, build subtext, give substance to characters that just doesn't happen in the first or second go-around. The story has to be completed to understand where the holes, the shallows, or the cracks are. Where characters are flat and plots overly-scripted. I self-edit a lot, then I read orally several times to someone. Then once the editor has had their hands on it, I read it orally again in addition to the screen edits. But to tell me I can over-edit is to talk to a brick wall. I don't believe there is such a thing as over-editing.

W.B.J. WILLIAMS (*The Garden at the Roof of the World*): I love editing and rewriting. I start with reading out loud, especially with dialogue, to ensure that it sounds natural and in character. My first drafts are always light on setting and heavy on dialogue. I do this deliberately because I want to know my characters well before writing the setting, which will necessarily reflect the character's viewpoint. Writing the dialogue first helps me learn and grow the characters and their relationships.

MARTIN ROSE (*Bring Me Flesh, I'll Bring Hell*): You're going to see a lot of red pen, and yours is just the beginning. I learned copy editing at a weekly paper. But copy editing is little stuff, grammar, spelling, and you want that manuscript polished, but that's not the key thing. The key thing is readability, sentence structure, and narrative. If this is a house, replacing drapes is no big deal. You want to make sure the beam is where it should be, or the whole thing falls apart. You don't want to be working on deadline and discover you need to write a whole new chapter because the one before it doesn't make sense without it. I usually write a story or a novel and then I return to it after several months. It's best if I forget everything about it. Every time I submit a story to a market, I read it over and I always find something that I feel should be changed or rewritten. Stories are never finished, but you want to learn how to throw out extraneous parts, and always try to put yourself in the shoes of the reader or the editor. You know the message you're trying to convey—they don't.

PEGGY A. WHEELER (*Chaco*): I can write a draft of an 80,000 word book in about three months, sometimes less or more, but then I spend a minimum of six to nine additional months incorporating edits and rewriting. I never send a manuscript to my publisher for pro editing until at least six other pairs of eyes have looked at it. I'm in critique groups. I share editing with other writers. I work with pro editors on my own. In my opinion, editing and rewrites are critical to good writing.

TODD KEISLING (*The Smile Factory*): Edits and revision are necessary parts of the writing process, even if it hurts—and I guarantee it will hurt. There's a good reason it's called "murdering your darlings."

LORI R. LOPEZ (*The Strange Tale of Oddzilla*): I do my own editing and will read over a piece three to four times. More if I'm still adding or making minor tweaks. With my first published novel and stories, I felt less confident about when they were finished. I have gone back years later and updated capitals in some of my books, lines, or paragraphs, for second editions. But I am generally satisfied after a few readings. Since I edit as I go, there is less to revise in this stage. Rarely anything to clean up. I will read it first to add details and lines I feel are missing. That's mostly what I do while editing. I fill in where it needs transitions to flow better. Where it needs elaboration. I might add touches of comedy here or there. Even my darkest horror has humor. I then read to look for plot holes and fill them in. To find inconsistencies. Each reading, I am able to focus more on the finer points as I grow satisfied with the flow, the wording, the story.

Others may write more in a day, faster, spending less time and getting more done. But they will remove a portion, whereas I will primarily add to the piece while I edit. It's a very different approach. Everyone has to find what works for them. There is no single way to write. I dislike the lists that say this is how to write. It isn't. I break a lot of the rules that many agree are the standards for writing well. I like to do things my way. I always have.

PAUL FLEWITT (*Poor Jeffrey*): I write all my first drafts in longhand, so I literally have pages of handwritten script in files all over the place. It takes more time, but I can't seem to find any flow if I'm working on a computer; I just can't type quickly enough to get the ideas from my head and onto the page. So, typing up the manuscript becomes my first edit pass. I'll embellish and polish the story as I type, adding phrases and building on the material that's already on the page, changing things that need to be changed and trying to improve the flow of the story. I generally spend a day or two every week typing up the pages written in the days preceding. Typing days are usually Mondays, which refreshes my mind on what I was doing before stopping work for the weekend.

GIL VALLE (*A Gathering of Evil*): I don't worry about perfect grammar or typos when I write my first draft. The only thing that needs to be perfect is the story and whether or not the various plots come together sensibly and logically. Once I have a solid first draft, I take a few days off and then I re-read it, looking for typos and anything that doesn't make sense in the plot. I often come up with a few new ideas as well, and when I do, I write them in and then fix whatever else needs to be fixed before or after the new additions.

After two or three re-reads, I focus on tightening up all of the literature. My co-author from [my memoir] Raw Deal is a professional writer, and he helps me a great deal with that. When he offers his feedback and corrections, I send it in to the publisher and await their edits and suggestions, and they all do a great job. Once I have the newest version back, I send it out to a couple of beta readers. They are so valuable to me, and they are honest with me. I hold their opinions and suggestions in the highest regard.   Writing a novel is far from a solo venture for me. There are many people behind the scenes who help, and I appreciate all of them. I strive for the final product to be perfect and free of typos. Typos are annoying and sloppy, and if one ever slips by in any of my books, I apologize to the reader.

JESSICA MCHUGH (*Rabbits in the Garden*): I don't edit as I write, so I know I have quite an undertaking ahead when I write "THE END" on a piece. Since I tend to follow characters more than plot, I sometimes don't know what the story is even truly about until the last third, so there's a lot to clean up. But for me, this is when the story really comes to life.

SCOTT M. BAKER (*Nazi Ghouls from Space*): The rewrite is not difficult for me; I usually make all the substantial changes during the initial drafting. Editing is where the book is made or broken, which is why I spend so much time on this part of the process. Mine goes through several stages as I review the manuscript for flow and readability, grammar and spelling errors, continuity issues, and finally, a search to replace repetitious words. I take as much time as I need for the rewriting/editing process because my readers deserve the best possible work I can give them.

J. STEFFY (*Evolution of a Monster*): Editing is based on the material. Most would be focused on grammar rules and spelling, but some need errors to create realism… Such as diaries… In rewriting, I write for a couple days, then go over it until I think it is good before writing more.

S.A. COSBY (*My Darkest Prayer*): The first draft is for me. The second draft is for the reader. I rarely rewrite the entire manuscript. But I will add or delete chapters as the story warrants. Sometimes, a section I think is extraordinary ends up on the cutting room floor because the reader doesn't really need it to enjoy the story.

J.C. MICHAEL (*Pandemonium*): When I started out, I naively believed that writers wrote, and editors edited. I genuinely believed that if I screwed up my grammar, it would be down to someone else to fix it. Yeah, right. Polishing a manuscript as much as you can is a necessary evil if you want to be taken serious and be published. Having said that, I still get my work back with fairly few grammatical corrections and errors that get picked up. It can be a pain, but it needs to be done. There is of course the other element where some editors will challenge the story itself and push you to change or improve it. I've been fortunate that, by and large, the end result has always been an improvement when I've had editors push me like that, and sometimes, I wish certain stories had been through that process. Oh, and the worst thing about editing? When you go through it all and then spot a mistake you've missed when you receive your author's copy. That sucks.

CHAD LUTZKE (*The Same Deep Water as You*): This is an area that should have no set rules as to the order of how it's done, other than at some point, editing needs to be done, and done well. Whether you edit as you write or you do a hideous first draft, warts and all, and then clean it up. They both work. But when your pen is down, your fingers off the keys, and "THE END" is staring at you from beneath the last line, it's time to go back and do it again. And probably more than once. More than twice. Printing off your manuscript in a different font and reading it aloud helps catch all those tiny errors that keep eluding you. And under this microscope don't be afraid to kill your darlings, taking out excessive wordage. There's a ton of it in there. Kill it. Kill it all, and make every word count.

EDWARD LEE (*White Trash Gothic*): It really is true what they say: most of writing is rewriting. It's just that computers make it faster and easier. Ideally, when I finish a book, I send it to some proof readers to check for typos, then wait a while, and line edit the whole thing myself. Of course, sometimes deadlines make that unfeasible. But if at all possible, put your first draft away for at least a month before you go back over it. And remember Stephen King's rule: Final Draft equals First Draft minus ten percent. It's sound advice.

RHONDA PARRISH (*Fae*): I work as an editor, and it's not because I'm a masochist—I love editing. And I'm good at it. First drafts, I'm not so good at. So for me, oftentimes the first draft is a race towards editing. All those memes you see that say writing is revising? They aren't wrong, but because everyone's system is different, they aren't necessarily right, either. I think every writer needs to have a set of fresh eyes look at their work before it goes out into the world (whether those eyes belong to an acquiring editor, a critique partner, a freelance editor, whatever) because as writers, we become blind to things in our own work, but I don't think every story needs umpteen revisions. Some do, sure. But there is such a thing as revising too much.

RICHARD GODWIN (*Savage Highway*): My process is always different. I write it and then take a break, then I edit. It may take four or five attempts, but I edit.

BARBARA ELLE (*Death in Vermillion*): As I close in completing *Death in Smoke,* I'm concentrating on the end goal—finishing with a manuscript that is approximately 90,000 words. The story has parallel storylines and enough complexity that it requires that length. I often do a lot of editing and rewriting as I write—I also spellcheck and keep a running word count.

My plan, when the second manuscript is complete, is to use beta readers this time around before sending the manuscript to my editor for proofreading and final continuity edits.

STEPHEN SPIGNESI (*Dialogues*): I'm pretty good with the first drafts of whatever I'm working on. I tend to revise as I write, probably because my OCD will not allow me to move on to the next sentence, paragraph, chapter, etc. until what I've written is the best it can be *at that moment*.
Of course I find things to revise and change when I do the big "complete manuscript" review and edit (always with input from my editor), but my first drafts aren't laden with typos, misspellings, etc. And most of my major thematic changes are done later, if at all. My first drafts are pretty clean in terms of them saying what I want them to say.

Once in a while, major changes will be needed, but that's uncommon. Any major changes usually involve cutting material. In my earlier days as a writer, I had a contract for an 80,000-word book, and I turned in 125,000 words. My editor—she was really very sweet about this egregiously unprofessional act by me—called and said, "Either you cut 40,000 words by Tuesday or we do it." That taught me a valuable lesson: don't mess with the terms of the contract without approval.

I usually have a vision of the final book that I work toward throughout the research, writing, and editing process. I knew precisely what my latest book *Stephen King, American Master* would look like before I even started working on it. In fact, I knew what my very first book—*Mayberry, My Hometown*—would look like before I had written a word. I strive for that clarity with my nonfiction book whenever possible.

GREG HICKEY (*The Friar's Lantern*): For me, rewriting is the hardest part of the writing process. Finishing the first draft of any new project is an incredible feeling. It always seems like all the work is behind me. Look at that giant stack of paper—I wrote all that! And some of it flowed so smoothly onto the page—I must have written some really great stuff! Then I read my first draft, and my excitement plummets. There are plot holes and tortured sentences everywhere. I've made grammar and spelling errors a third-grader wouldn't make. It's hard to know where to begin to salvage something out of this linguistic catastrophe.

At this lowest point, rewriting can look overwhelming. It helps to make a plan and focus on doing a little bit at a time. Rewrite a dysfunctional scene one day. Fill in a plot hole the next. Just like writing a little bit every day adds up over time, the same is true of rewriting. And then the process repeats itself all over again with the next draft.

M. NAIDOO (*Where Sleeping Lies Lie*): I actually look forward to rewrites and editing. They are my excuse for turning out a first draft that makes me cringe. Rewriting and editing can easily take longer than writing the initial draft since I am a hopeless perfectionist and the master of second-guessing. Aside from the obvious proofreading and line edit, I don't think a manuscript is ever truly done. There just comes the point when you have to decide that it's enough or risk over-editing. I trust my editor to reign me in.

BEN OHMART (*The Rerun of Dracula*): I wish someone had really made me believe that writing is a collaborative process. I knew it was for TV and film writing, but even for novels, you have to listen to your publisher and editor, or nothing great will happen. Even if they release what you write, if you're a baby and have to have your writing your way, if you don't listen to the people who have been at it longer, you're going to float away in a sea of Kindle that is as endless as it is full of garbage covers. And no one today has the patience to endlessly browse to try to find a gem in the dark hole in the earth that is the Kindle Fiction category.

Having a good editor is key. While it is easier and sometimes popular to say "make it better," you want an editor who tells you How. Finding the right people to help you will take time. It might take more effort than writing the stuff. But it's really important, especially when you're starting out or still eating Ramen noodles.

B.R. STATEHAM (*Murder Is Our Business*): I'm not fond of the word 'rewriting.' To me, that sounds like someone writes something, doesn't like it, so they tear it up and begin again. I tinker. I write it the first time, and then I tinker with it, changing something here, a word there, and try to give it better clarity or more visual imagery. I really believe the soul of writing comes out the first time. In the first effort. You can make some adjustments. But in essence, the whole should be good enough to continue working with it.

DOUGLAS BRODE (*Sweet Prince: The Passion of Hamlet*): There are only two basic rules…one, already stated, "a writer writes." No matter what. The other? ALL GOOD WRITING IS REWRITING. When I was young, I had ridiculously romantic ideas about writing. Girls, too, only that's a different subject for a different day. Get a reality check! I then believed in inspiration, and making matters worse, I wrote in LONGHAND. That's the worst thing you can do. There's something about seeing the words on paper, in your own way of lettering, that makes the process feel like a religious experience and that the piece should remain pure and untouched. BULLSHIT! That's strictly for amateurs who like to pretend they are writers. Which is what I once was, but not any longer. Work on a word processor always. That makes the words feel objective—you don't mind going over them and rewriting them. Also, consider working with a partner. Most often, whenever I have done so, the experience was horrible. We tried to compose together and argued and argued. If you are a writer with a strong storyline and characters in mind, you don't want to work with a writer similar to that…in my case, several years ago, I asked my son Shaun to collaborate with me. I could never have guessed how wonderful it would be. Right now, I'm down in my Florida beach house writing new stuff for the third volume of our Planet Jesus Trilogy—the concept was entirely mine. So were the storyline, characters, and themes. Then I send the chapter that I wrote that day to Shaun in San Antonio via email. He sits down and reads it, knows what I want to say, and—here's what makes it work—then rewrites it in order that the words express, to the best ability, what I meant to convey. Very often, as a writer, you are too subjective about your work—too close to it—to know if you succeeded or failed in getting things across. Shaun reads it over, knows me like a book, and immediately realizes that the choice of a verb in one sentence may be "okay," but there's a far better one. Or that I used three adjectives (I tend to overwrite horribly!) where two, maybe even one, maybe even none would do. We go over this on the phone (together when we are in the same place) and decide together which of his changes we want to use—usually ninety percent of them. He takes my book and turns it into what I wanted it to be but couldn't reach on my own. Also, take advice from writers you respect—meaning the ones who don't fawn over you or tear you down but critically want to help. One of my best friends, the writer-filmmaker Rod Lurie, once commented that I always take things too far. In a paragraph, I have one more sentence than necessary. In a chapter, one more paragraph. In a book, one too many chapters. Though he told me this twenty years ago, I never let it out of my mind. I read over everything I do thinking of that. Not that I always 'slavishly' take his advice. But looking at what I did through his eyes, nine out of ten times, I do cut.

Also—key rule—always say as much as you can in as few words as possible. Less is more. Read Hemingway to get a sense of this. Get to the heart of the matter, as Graham Greene (the British author, not the Native American actor) would say.

Advice For Aspiring Writers 4

STEWART O'NAN (*Snow Angels*): My best advice for aspiring writers is to try to stay close to your characters, to live with them and come to know them better than the people you love, and still be surprised by their lives.

MICHELLE BOWSER (*A Gross Miscellany*): Advice? Just the cliches. They are cliches for a reason.

ANDY RAUSCH (*Bloody Sheets*): My biggest pieces of advice are probably obvious ones, but they are always believe in yourself and read. Read lots of books by lots of authors in lots of different genres. Reading the writing of great writers is like a master class in writing, but reading the works of terrible authors can be just as educational because they show you what you don't want to do.

MARK SLADE (*A Six Gun & the Queen of Light*): The best advice I think I ever got was to just complete the story the best way you know how. Stay focused. Maybe do research on the time period you are writing about, read a book on a subject that has to do with your story, or even watch a film that is connected to the story. Try to stay on a schedule, whatever that schedule is. Write whatever you can, whether it's 500 words or 10,000. I think it's best to keep a little tucked away; don't push yourself or you'll run out of gas. To be honest, no advice can be the best advice on writing. You either feel you have to do it, or writing isn't your bag. You'll do what it takes to get your voice heard.

GARY VINCENT (*Darkened Hills*): Write without regards to worrying about what people will *think* about you. If the story requires you to go into those dark places, well, go there! I honestly think that much of today's writing is an attempt to be politically correct or sensitive—coming from a place of worry that a writer might get criticized. So what? The critics will come no matter how good a writer you are, so you might as well write the story the way it should be written and not some piece to appeal to those few opinions you're worried about upsetting. In the end, it really doesn't matter what people think as long as you feel you've done your best and that you told the story that you wanted the way you wanted to tell it.

BECKY NARRON (short-story writer, numerous anthologies): Read, read, read. Write, don't stop ever. Have people read your writing, and listen to what they tell you. It will make you a better writer. Don't throw anything away. Never throw things away. Follow your heart, and write what you know. Above all else, be true to yourself. Don't let others sway you into their mold. No one can write like you except you!

JOE R. LANSDALE (*Bubba Ho-Tep*): Read a lot. Sit down and write and try to write enough a day to know you've done it, but not so much you dread the work. It should be fun. That doesn't mean it can't be hard, but it should still be a joy, and finishing daily should make the rest of your day feel better. It's like exercise, you have to do it regularly to maintain the flow and to develop the ability to show up and do it without turning it into a chore. I enjoy writing, not just having written.

CHRIS ROY (*Her Name Is Mercie*): A body that isn't constantly challenged will become slow and ugly. A mind that isn't constantly challenged will become slow and stupid. Your physical ability affects your mental performance. If you want to produce some truly sharp pieces of fiction, you need discipline to endure the years. Get your ass in shape, and your mind will follow.

GRAHAM MASTERSON (*The Manitou*): Be totally original. Don't copy any other writer, no matter how successful they are. Your own voice is what your readers want to hear. Keep writing, even when your stories have been rejected, but do listen to the criticism of experienced editors. And always start the day with moisturizer. As a professional writer you are going to be squinching your eyes at a screen for years on end, and you don't want to end up wrinkly.

ELKA RAY (*Saigon Dark*): There's only one reason to write: because you have to. If you don't have a weird, burning need to tell stories, why would you put so much work into something that will, more likely than not, pay less by the hour than flipping burgers? But if you need to write: go for it. Keep at it, you'll get better. Writing is a craft, like wood-working. You're not some mystical cravat-wearing scribe throwing out scintillating pears of wisdom. You're a woodworker.

EDDIE GENEROUS (*Radio Run*): Stop waiting to have your ducks aligned, and just write some stories. It's okay if your first novel never sells. Write a second one. It's okay if that one doesn't sell either. Write ten more.

BRIAN BARR (*Dark Ripple: When Lovecraft Met Crowley*): Learn as much as you can, study from various sources, and never get caught up in one person's prejudices when it comes to writing. Open yourself up to various styles, and find what works for you. Write the kind of stories you want to write. Have fun.

JOHN W. WOOD (*White Crow*): Read, read, read, and then write, write, write. Be aware of your surroundings, conversations, how people walk, etc. Writers today have such an advantage over those writers in the past. We have Google for reference and computers and programs that tell us how bad we are at punctuation and spelling. But, in the end, it has to be edited by someone other than yourself; never ever, be your own editor.

G. MIKI HAYDEN (*Strings*): Make sure your presentation is competitive. Sorry to say, but these days, you generally will need a pre-publication edit from someone like me. I'm pretty darn sure you've made a lot of novice writing errors even if you've been writing for years. That's just the reality, and despite the face that publication is a wild crapshoot, to gamble on your story, you need to spend the dollars first.

JENNIFER BROWN (*Hate List*): Dabbling is fine if you want to keep writing as a hobby. But if you want to make it your career, you have to treat it like one. You have to discipline yourself to show up to work. You have to commit to learning about the business—and continuing to learn, as it's an ever-changing market. Read every book on writing that you can get your hands on. Go to every conference you can get to—and schedule critiques or pitches with agents and editors while you're there. Talk to writers about their habits; get their advice. Read books in the genre you're interested in writing. Join critique groups and online writing groups. Write every day. Read every day. And, most importantly, submit your work! Submit small stuff to build up your bylines, and submit bigger stuff when it's ready.

And start working on your resilience, because this business requires it. Rejection happens. And happens and happens and happens. And it stings. Revisions can sting. Reviews can sting. It is easy to get discouraged. Go ahead and take some time to lick your wounds, if you must, but make that time short (no longer than a weekend for me), and then get back in the game. You can't win if you're not playing!

DAVID CLARK (*Game Master*): Always write about what you love. Don't just author a story you think is pop-culture/marketable. Write on the subject you will enjoy. The story will just flow if you love the subject.

SAMANTHA BRYANT (*Face the Change: Menopausal Superheroes*): There is no right way to do this. Art is individual. It's a long voyage, and how it's best to navigate will change over time and circumstance. Finding your way will require trial and error and a great deal of reflection and analysis. Don't worry about what anyone says about how or why or what you "should" be doing. Come with a heart to learn and explore and enjoy the ride!

CHRIS MILLER (*A Murder of Saints*): Try to write every day if you can. Don't beat yourself up if you can't. Read as much as possible. Studying the craft from other writers can be interesting, but rarely helpful. We all do it differently, we all have different processes, and trying to mimic someone else's will likely not work. You have to develop your own, and the only way to do that is to sit down at the keyboard and just start doing it. Meet as many folks in the industry as you can, and network to the best of your ability. Connect with readers, beta readers, other writers, small press publishers, editors, proofreaders, agents, whomever you can. Learn from them. Get a thick skin. Take criticism and apply it. Not all criticism is accurate, but a lot will be. Learn to spot the difference and consider the source. Dismiss what's wrong, apply what's right, and grow in your craft. And don't forget to read, read, read.

MAX ALLAN COLLINS (*Road to Peridition*): Don't limit yourself. Learn the different requirements of various storytelling forms—novels aren't movies, movies aren't comics, etc. If you can, write in every genre that interests you, although that can be an uphill battle—editors and agents will try to pigeonhole you—readers, too. Give yourself plenty of options, if you're trying to make a living at this.

THOMAS GUNTHER (*The Big Book of Bootleg Horror: Volume Four*): Write, write, write, and submit, and submit, and submit! I know so many closet-writers. They're so afraid of rejection and tend to talk themselves out of submitting anything. Like it's a mystery club or something. No one gets any good at writing unless they're writing constantly and putting themselves out there constantly. Rejection is normal. I used to collect rejection letters. I probably still have some. Occasionally, editors would do me the favor of dropping some constructive criticism. I didn't always appreciate it back then, but it proved very useful later on, and I am grateful. Rejection is good. It means you have to work toward improvement, and that's the secret joy of writing. So, keep working at it, keep writing, and write about anything. Here's a good exercise: write about the most boring, mundane thing or chore—one you loathe—and describe it in such a way that the reader can appreciate your pain. I actually ended up using this method in a story that begins with the protagonist picking up dog poop! And, if nothing else, always keep a pen and paper or a tape recorder handy. One never knows when an idea will strike.

JOHN PALISANO (*Night of 1,000 Beasts*): There's the classic time-worn response to read every day, read widely, and write daily, as well. Writing is a muscle. Staying in shape physically has stayed the same for ages, too. Work off more calories than you put in. Vary what you do. Same for writing. You can use pen and paper, typewriter, computer, composition book, smart phone, dictation sofware—anything that works to help transcribe your story from your imagination into something shareable and tangible. No matter what, there are no real shortcuts to just putting in the work of doing so. If it burns inside you, then do it and don't give up.

MAXWELL BAUMAN (*The Anarchist Kosher Cookbook*): Join a newspaper as a copy editor. It will help improve your grammar and fact-checking/research skills. Even if you're writing fiction, historical or otherwise, it's important to get all the details right. Sure, you have some leeway when you're creating the world of your story, but your readers are smart and will appreciate the extra level of attention. And never forget that your time is valuable. Creating an outline can help you be more productive. Keep doing free-writes, but outlines will help you stay on track, and you won't find yourself 50,000 words deep and not knowing how to end the story.

BEV VINCENT (*Flight or Fright*): Given the opportunity, I have two kinds of advice for aspiring writers: first, don't be in a huge rush to get something—anything—published. That's when mistakes get made. Mistakes like sending something out before it's ready or compromising your career in the name of Getting Something In Print. We all fall prey to that temptation in the early days of our writing careers—the lure of seeing our names in print. If a story is good, it will keep. I've published stories that I wrote five years ago, and they're still as valid today as they were when I first wrote "The End." There's a feeling, I think, that if you don't get it out NOW, it will somehow perish. Most fiction doesn't have an expiration or sell-by date. Sure, you might need to update a few details in an old story, but the story itself will most likely still be pertinent. Aim high, right from the beginning. Don't fall prey to the lure of getting "paid" by exposure. Exposure isn't payment—it's how people who get lost in the woods die. Steer clear of payment by royalty only—those projects almost never generate income. I know it's not about payment, it's about the art… but if you want to be well-published—by which I mean published in a place that people respect and where a lot of people will see your work—be picky about where you submit and be patient.

Secondly, and on a completely different subject: don't spend too much of your life sitting down. If there's one thing I'd go back in time and tell a younger me, it would be to sit less. Sitting is hard on your back, and when you get older, you'll pay for it! That's why I use the kangaroo desk. If only I had adopted it earlier!

PAUL D. BRAZILL (*Cold London Blues*): Enjoy yourself, it's later than you think!

TRAVIS WALLACE (*Clues*): Find friends who also write. Unless they are frauds, they will understand your struggles with either the words or confidence, and it works to share experiences or just provide an empathetic ear. Hopefully, they are honest and trustworthy so when they tell you something you have written or thinking about writing sucks, it is a confirmation of what you were thinking yourself.

PAUL HEATLEY (*An Eye for an Eye*): Do it every day. It's the best piece of advice I ever read, and I didn't heed it at first. I balked at it, but it's what works for me, and truth be told, I think it's what will work for everyone else, too. Another thing that works for me is planning. If you have an outline, even if it's just a rough idea of what you're trying to do, where you want the story to go, and if you study and acquaint yourself with that before you set down to work, you're far less likely to write yourself into a corner with no foreseeable way out.

BRIAN JAMES LANE (*Fright Feast*): Completing the first novel is a monumental step and one that can destroy barriers of self-doubt and worry. You just have to get through one, and the rest come much more easily. My first completed novel felt like I had shed the shackles of "can't" and "never". It was liberating. I never again had to worry about if I could because I had.

When I first started novel writing, I did so as a participant in National Novel Writing Month. The community and the deadlines helped me to finish what I had started. I liked it so much, I completed a NANO project each year for a decade. It is a good way to place your toes in the water of the craft before jumping into the deep end (and possibly drown)!

One day, I realized I didn't need to sprint to finish. I could jog. Hell, I could walk. It isn't a race. It's an odyssey. I grasped that concept that the fun is in the writing, not the finished product. When I started enjoying the process, it wasn't a matter of completion. It was a matter of the act of writing being pleasurable. I believe this is a natural maturation for the author. I write because I like to write. It's fun.

An athlete doesn't run a marathon the first time they try. They must train for it. Each time they run, they get better. This is true for writing, as well. You need to have the discipline to continue writing even if the finished piece isn't terrific. You are getting better as you go. Keep running!

CARMEN AMATO (*Cliff Diver*): Don't fall in love with your first draft. It won't be good and that's okay. It isn't supposed to be. Learn to be a ruthless editor of your own work, and aim for a high quality product.

PAUL TREMBLAY (*Head Full of Ghosts*): Read, read, and read. Read widely. Read outside your genre too. Also, if you can, find a group of like-minded writers/friends who are about the same level (experience, publishing history) as you are. It doesn't have to be a writing group, per se, but it helps to have friends with whom you can commiserate, share the struggle, etc. I have a good friend I talk to once a week on the phone, and we shoot the shit mostly, but we do talk writing, our frustrations, and our successes, and it's an important, battery re-charging part of my writing life.

LILY LAMB (*The Dowling House*): Being a writer is like jumping into the deep ocean—keep swimming!

CHARLES LYNNE (*What Screams in the Dark*): Get a thought in your head, and write it down. No matter what it is. That will get the creative part of your mind working. Also, if you don't write it down immediately, you might lose it. No idea is a bad idea. I read something once that made a lot of sense. Someone had the idea to put sharks in a tornado. They not only made that happen once, they had sequels.

MIKE PURFIELD (*In a Blackened Sky Where Dreams Collide*): Ditch the ego, don't be afraid to learn, and have discipline. Not everything you write is going to be perfect, and not everything you write everyone is going to love. As a writer, you are going to write hundreds of pieces. A handful of those items will click with someone, and out of those people, you will gain some fans who will read your catalog and your future works. Be grateful for that in this over-saturated business. In the long run, there are those that give up after a few books because they don't find the riches and fans that they think they deserve, and they give up. If you are a writer, then you will love writing. You will love the challenge of sitting there and coming up with new and interesting stories. That is the high. That is enough.

Read those how-to books, but don't make them your bible. They can give you the basics for your beginning works, but they cannot teach you how to be original. Think about it. How can a writer teach you how to be original? Only you can write something original. Originality comes from creativity, and that comes from you. The best way to be original is to break rules. Another way is to know your history. Read in and out of your genre. You don't have to read all outside genres, but if you write horror and you like middle-reader books, then that's awesome. Read them. My point is, learning other ways to tell stories is important to your creativity.

Also reading older fiction. The past is so important. Not just the standard classics, but classics in your genre as well. Most likely, you will find you are not so original and that someone has come up with your ideas before. You can learn to take those previous ideas and push them further. Make them your own.

Keep writing. Don't stop. Start off writing short stories until you feel you've mastered it. If you feel comfortable, send them out or publish them. When you're ready, try writing a novel. Don't spend years writing a novel. Do it in a few months. When that novel is done, do another. Or rewrite it from scratch (from word one) if you bungled it up. Or do more short stories. Practice. Don't do drafts. Build your muscles and skills in storytelling. If all goes well, you will have a muscular brain.

ISOBEL BLACKTHORN (*Clarissa's Warning*): The only advice I have is what was told to me. Write every day for a minimum of three hours. Read, read, read, and as you read, study the way the author has crafted their work. Read literary fiction for the handling of themes and characterization, read good horror and thrillers because they will teach you a lot about style and pacing. Crime is where the plotters hang out. Fantasy for world building. Just read, but read actively as though you are studying for an exam. You can sign up for a writing course if you want, and it will teach you the same. Also, learn the basic rules of grammar. Then, when you are ready to start writing, imagine a person a little bit brighter than you, and write to impress them. In other words, be prepared to strive and strive. Be prepared for a long, hard road filled with setbacks and knock-backs and endless rejection. Probably wise not to give up the day job. We can't all be Lee Child or Stephen King.

BOB VAN LAERHOVEN (*Return to Hiroshima*): Find professional help. Assemble a team of psychiatrists around you 24/7. Or go binge drinking until you've utterly destroyed each morsel of every memory about yearning to write. And if these kill or cure remedies don't work, when this horrible disease keeps on eating you alive, then, by all means, go for it: write, write, write, rewrite, rewrite, rewrite… But, for God's sake, be funnier than I am.

HEYWOOD GOULD (*Fort Apache, The Bronx*): We all dream of fame and fortune. But do it for love, or don't do it.

DAVID L. TAMARIN (*BOLO: Sociopaths on a Rampage*): When you are ready to submit to magazines, be familiar with the magazines. You need to know the right places to submit your fiction. A lot of rejection is simply because of where you submitted a story.

BRET MCCORMICK (*Headhunters from Outer Space*): Writing, like marriage, requires commitment. Most of the people I meet who say they want to write really just mean they want to talk about writing and fantasize about being a writer. I liken these folks to the lonely woman who reads five romance novels a week, but will never have a real, successful romantic relationship. Or the horny guy who habitually cruises nightclubs and gets lots of ass, but has no intention of building a lasting bond with anyone. (I'm intimately acquainted with the spurious merits of promiscuity, but it never produces anything worthy of admiration.) Both writing and relationships are lots of work, and many of us don't have a strong enough desire to commit. Consequently, most marriages end in divorce, and most novels become incomplete files or stacks of paper that end up in the scrap heap as recycled paper or data on discarded electronic devices.

Write every day if you want to be a writer. It's just like being a doctor or an athlete. The more you do it, the better you get. Also, don't beat yourself up. Write what you write, and let it accumulate like trees in a forest. Some will be unremarkable scrub bushes, but if you write consistently, some will be majestic oaks. You may even find a giant redwood in your forest. Let your forest be what it is. Don't try to hide the lesser trees or apologize for them. They're your children, your creations, let them all exist as worthy of being just because they are yours. Own them.

AUTUMN CHRISTIAN (*Girl Like a Bomb*): Write until your little hands become purple and bruised from striking the keyboard so many times and so hard. Finish everything, even if it sucks. If you keep finishing things, you'll probably eventually stop sucking. Be open, both your eyes and your heart. Take criticism as what it really is - an opportunity to become better, not a blow to your essence or ego. Stop talking so much about your writing. Research the industry because there are a lot of snakes, and also because you want to portray yourself as competent and well-informed. Stop expending creative energy on building your fantasy life in your head if only you were a great, famous writer, and just write, because it's the only way to get there.

Oh, and no drinking soda, watching television, hot showers, or masturbating. Those are all detrimental to your creative power. (I am just kidding about that last part. I just wanted to scare someone.)

KURT BELCHER (*Spiders & Stardust*): Write, read, write, read, write, read… I know everyone says that, but that doesn't make it less true. And read all kinds of things: novels, short stories, the news, nonfiction, comic books, screenplays… Be an active participant in the reading, rather than passively reading for fun. Read with a critical eye towards story beats and dialogue. Break down how things work in everything that you read and watch, and try to think how you'd apply those things to your own work. This is true of written material and watching movies. Everything is fuel for improving your work.

KASEY PIERCE (*Pieces of Madness*): There's a lot of power is being an author. It means you're not the person who'll forever say "Ya know, I was gonna write a book once..." Every few seconds, someone somewhere has a great idea. An author is the one who steps from the sea of idea men to not only write it, but have the balls to put it in a publisher's hands and say "Here. I created something I'm passionate about, and here's why you should feel passionate about it, too..."

Also, don't be too attached to a piece. Once you've put it out there, it's subject for readers and critics to praise or tear apart. Take both the glory and the guillotine, grow, and move on. If our next book is our final opus, what the hell was the point of all this? If you possess a willingness to listen to your editors and your publishers, then your next book will always be your greatest.

DEV JARRETT (*Loveless*): Aside from advice on the actual craft of writing, my advice is simply this: keep doing it. Persist. You'll need a thick skin sometimes, and an infinite supply of optimism, but even when you have those bad days writing, or those bad e-mails from editors and agents, keep at it. Learn from your mistakes, and keep writing.

MELISSA KEIR (*Cowboy, Mine*): First and foremost, this isn't a sprint. Becoming an author takes time. The process doesn't happen overnight. While it seems like it does because you hear about a person like JK Rowling who wrote a story and became a media sensation, you quickly find out that to create a quality book, you must write and edit, then edit more and write more, then format, order a cover, and finally you get your book out there. But that's only the beginning…

Additionally, while writing appears to be something you'd get rich off of, it's not. Even if you are lucky to get your book written, edited, and finally published…now you have to sell it, which takes more time and money. You need to share your book with readers through a variety of outlets from newsletters and social media, book signings, and giveaways. Amazon and the other retailers are going to discount your book and give you only a portion of the sales because they are handling the purchase, distribution, and taxes for your book. Unless it's going to make them a ton of money, they won't even promote your book.

Like being a parent or a teacher, many people believe being an author is easy. After all, everyone writes. But an author has determination not to give up and the tenacity to see the writing through to the end. They are willing to let someone else rip their baby up and help create a better one. An author is open to learning their craft so the stories pull at the emotions of the reader and engage their senses. Most of all, they write because they love it and wouldn't want to do anything different.

DAVID OWAIN HUGHES (*Brain Damage*): *Never* give up. Persist. When the odds seem stacked against you, dig your heels in, and don't ever let bad reviews, rejections, or words of discouragement defeat you. Grow a thick skin, and prepare for a long, often thankless, journey. Being or becoming a writer isn't an easy task, and you'll learn something new every day. Also, listen to advice given to you by seasoned authors. Don't make the mistake of thinking you know it all. Above all else, don't let *anything* stop you. I saw this quote by William Goldman which sums up being an author: "Writing is finally about one thing: going into a room alone and doing it. Putting words on paper that have never been there in quite that way before. And although you are physically by yourself, the haunting demon never leaves you, that demon being the knowledge of your own terrible limitations, your hopeless inadequacy, the impossibility of ever getting it right. No matter how diamond-bright your ideas are dancing in your brain, on paper they are earthbound. If you're trying a screenplay, you know it's never going to be Bergman. ….. But if you're a writer, that's what you must do, and in order to accomplish anything at all, at the rock bottom of it all is your confidence. You tell yourself lies and you force them into belief: Hey, you suckers, I'm going to do it this one time. I'm going to tell you things you never knew. I've—got—secrets!" (From *Adventures in the Screen Trade*, 1983.)

JEFF PARSONS (*The Captivating Flames of Madness*): Have fun! Keep at it. Start small. Try to get published in a small press "for the love of it" magazine. Learn what you can from critiques, but also remember that everyone's style is different. You've got to adapt to what editors want, but in the end, you've also got to be yourself to let your best work shine forth. Eventually, you'll get that first story published, and it'll all be worth it. You're a published author—you'll feel great. Also, if one editor doesn't accept your story, resubmit it elsewhere. Your story may not fit with the anthological feeling they're looking to create, or it may not play well with other stories, or, gee whiz, maybe it was just bad timing. I once resubmitted a story six times to a variety of different places before it got accepted (hello, at a professional rate, too). Don't give up!

MICHAEL CIESLAK (*Desolation: 21 Tales for Tails*): My primary advice would be: Don't be an aspiring writer. Be a writer. Sit down and write. Do the work. Don't sit on the finished project, send it out. I don't actually have a copy of my first acceptance letter. I think it may actually have been an e-mail which is now lost to the ether. I do, however, have my first rejection letter framed and hanging over my desk. That was a turning point, when I first had the courage to send something out.

Do what you can to learn from other writers. This may come from actually spending time with them in writing groups, at conventions, in classrooms, but more commonly, it comes from reading. Find writers whose work you enjoy and see what they do well. Find writers whose work you did not enjoy and figure out why. While it is important to know what is happening in your own genre, don't be afraid to venture outside it.

Cultivate a group of beta readers, people who will give you honest responses to your work. Also, people who will be willing to do this for the price of a beer or a dinner or something that won't break the bank. Your mom is probably not going to be a good beta reader for you because she doesn't want to hurt your feelings. (My mom on the other hand, is an English major who will call out my mistakes, so she is an excellent beta reader). I have two groups of people who look over my work, one who is familiar with genre fiction and one who is not. The first can identify where something reads too much like someone else's book and can offer critiques based upon their knowledge of other similar books. The second can let me know what does and doesn't work on a story structure level without getting swept up by whatever cool idea I've presented.

Finally, as noted earlier, write.

PHIL PRICE (*Unknown*): Believe in yourself. That's the best advice I can give. If you think you're good enough, go for it! Don't hold back, and don't keep it secret. Tell family and friends about your writing. Many authors I know don't get as much support from these quarters as they would like. So shout it from the rooftops.

Don't rush your writing. It's really tempting to try and blast a book out, or blast a chapter out because the sexy chapter is next. Readers will pick up on that. Savor your writing. It's a slow process, enjoy every word.

Another thing that I think is really important is social media. When a new writer is planning to embark on a career/hobby as an author, they need to start building a following. I didn't, and it took a while to get traction. Word of warning, though: it will take time. Don't just expect hundreds of people who love you. Build it up slowly. And for god's sake, don't just post about your books, that is a real turn off. Post about yourself, have fun, and get to know the readers. Do giveaways and fun games, getting readers involved. Look at Facebook, Twitter, Instagram, etc., and build a brand that is a bit unique and quirky. I hope I have done that. If anyone disagrees, please call my PA. Oh wait. I don't have a PA.

JESSE DEDMAN (*The Master's Torment*): Don't expect it to be easy. You can aspire to be a big-name author, and maybe that'll happen, but don't expect it to be that easy. The industry is tougher. More and more people are coming in, and as a result, the chance a big publisher will pick you up is smaller.

However, there are so many ways to get your story out there, and with a persistent marketing, you'll be able to connect with readers. If you take on publishing yourself, just remember that you are your own gatekeeper, and you can't blame the market.

JAMES WATTS (*Them*): Read as much as possible, preferably in the genre you prefer to write. There are a lot of people out there in writing groups who will say reading is not essential to writing. Well, they are drinking Drano. Reading is a key factor in writing effectively. Work hard, and write every day or as much as you can. You will get rejections, so don't get discouraged by that. Keep pushing and submitting. Never give up.

A.P. SESSLER (*The First Suitor*): Don't think about writing. Write. Don't keep all the ideas in your head thinking you'll always remember them because time and life will slowly creep in and take up space, pushing those ideas further and further into some obscure spot in your brain attic. And since most aspiring writers are presumably younger than myself, know that the earlier you get started on writing and submitting to publishers, the higher chance you have at success coming sooner rather than later. So stop procrastinating and do it!

JASON PARENT (*A Life Removed*): You will get many rejections. They should not dishearten you. We all get them. And when you get that first acceptance, you will forget about all the rejections that came before it.

STANLEY B. WEBB (short-story writer, numerous anthologies): Do not worry about your product. Write because you want to. Do not take rejections personally. Rejections are not judgments.

WADE H. GARRETT (*Pigs: An Extreme Horror Novella*): Write what you enjoy.

RICHARD CHRISTIAN MATHESON (*Scars and Other Distinguishing Marks*): I rewrite everything, 50 or more times—major and slight adjustments. Tighten dialogue. Streamline prose. I edit with ruthless but rhythmic intent. When I can think of nothing else to add or subtract, I am done… until the next time I read it. It's a tightrope and seductive. Over-editing can stop the heart of what you've written.

ANDREW LENNON (*Bound*): Just write! So many people want to write, but they're too scared to get going. Perhaps too scared that they'll be judged or too scared that they'll fail. But here's the thing, if you don't try, then failure is your only option, isn't it?

Pay attention to reviews, but don't take them personally. You can write the biggest masterpiece of our time, but there will always be someone who doesn't like it. Art is subjective; you can't please everyone. Positive reviews are great, and they make you feel great. Negative reviews, however, are often a lot more constructive. If a reviewer has taken the time to highlight issues with your book, then pay attention to those issues, work on them, and try to improve for your next piece. One of the best feelings I've ever had was when I won a reviewer over, someone who originally didn't like my work at all, but I paid attention, I tried my best and improved, and now they are full of positive things to say about my work. That, to me, is a great achievement.

Try to write as often as you can. As I stated previously in this book, I have far too many slumps. When I write often, my writing is better, and it makes me feel good. Discipline is a very big thing.

Finally, don't try and cut corners. Do not assume you can edit yourself. Do not try and make your own cover. Readers spot these books a mile away, homemade covers look tacky, and they'll be avoided. If you do have a good cover, and you've managed to entice your reader, and then the book is filled with errors, you're going to lose them for future books. There's a reason editors get paid for their work. What they do is their own talent. Trust them and trust me, you need them.

PEGGY CHRISTIE (*Hell Hath No Fury*): Buy stock in coffee and booze. If that's not your thing, then just keep writing. Don't write for anyone else but you. Audiences are fickle; trends are short-lived; agents, managers, directors, celebrities, friends, strangers, that weird guy on the bus who keeps smelling his fingers—they don't know everything, and their advice isn't always spot on. So, write what makes you happy, develop your own writing habits and environment, and above all, write what *you* like. I promise, there is a reader out there waiting for the story only you can tell.

CHRISTOPH PAUL (*A Confederacy of Hot Dogs*): There is the obvious read and write a ton and explore all the genres, which is always the best advice. What I can add to it is also work with editors; honestly a good editor has probably more value than most MFA programs. Also befriend talented writers on social media or in your area. They will share the best books and presses and will help you expand your network.

BILLY CHIZMAR (*Widow's Point*): Just write. Write and write and write until your fingertips bleed and your wrists feel like the pistons of a rusted Chevy T-Bird. Let the stories sit in your desk drawer, and come back later. Read them. Find out what your obsessions are, be them topical, mechanical, or thematic. Do a lot of your stories involve religious cult? Do you really enjoy playing with language or syntax? Are you often writing into an underlying theme of betrayal? Embrace those things. They are what you love, so love them, but be skeptical. Recognize your patterns, embrace them, but don't be afraid to diverge from your personal beaten path into the wild expanse outside your comfort zone. There's cool stuff out there. You might just fall in love all over again.

JOE X. YOUNG (short-story writer, numerous anthologies): Write for love. If you think you are going to make millions, then good luck to you, as it's closer to the truth to say that the majority of writers can't afford to give up their day jobs, so write because you love doing it and not because you love the idea of money or fame.

If you want to be a writer, you really need to be a reader. Almost everyone says it, but they say it for a reason, because reading is part of the education required to hone your craft.

Write. There's no alternative. There are a lot of people who will call themselves writers on social media, and when asked what they have written, they have nothing they can readily point you toward. An actual writer actually writes.

Develop the hide of a rhino. You will face criticism. Nobody has ever written anything which has pleased one hundred percent of the readers one hundred percent of the time, so you need to be prepared to have your work trashed by critics and/or readers. If you don't think you can handle being told that your masterpiece sucks, then you should quit now.

Find an editor you can trust. Research them carefully. Look for a proven track record of successful clients from the quality end of the spectrum. There are plenty of people calling themselves editors who will charge you moderate to enormous sums of money for work they don't carry out.

Never pay to be published. The only costs you should have are those incurred when self-publishing, as you'll need to pay for covers, formatting, editing, etc.

The advice I give myself every day is to never give up. If you love what you do and care enough about it, then nothing will prevent you from at the very least completing a story. I have plenty of reasons why I could quit, and I have things which slow me down, but nothing this side of the grim reaper will stop me. Perseverance pays off, and the satisfaction I have had from seeing stories of mine in print and qualifying as a member of the Horror Writers Association has been well worth every obstacle I have faced.

DEAN M. DRINKEL (*Demonologica Biblica*): I can actually speak from experience in the fact that I mentored a younger (and aspiring) writer on one of my film projects. I tried (I'm not saying I was entirely successful) to be to him what I needed when I was his age and my first book came out. Back then, I'd sat by the door waiting for Hollywood to come knocking, and it didn't, so I ended up cleaning aeroplanes for a living. It took me a little while to find my place in the creative world, and I really wish I had someone who could have mentored and guided me, introducing me to people. I hate networking with a passion, but it is so important, as our industry is based more upon who you know rather than what you know. Yes, you can have an amazing talent, but if you have no one to help you realize that talent, then it's not going to happen for you. I've never been a fan of writing groups, but I can see that working for some people. Social media can really help you as long as you treat it respectfully. Finally, I'd say (and this is really important)—never bite the hand of someone who helps you. It is such a small industry, and you can't make enemies.

EVANS LIGHT (*Black Door*): Ask avid readers who don't mind hurting your feelings if your work is good. Not everything you write should be released for sale. If enough honest people say your writing needs improvement, believe them and keep practicing until feedback becomes positive.

JAMES H. LONGMORE (*Pede*): I could be awfully twee with this one and say "Don't do it!" But as anyone with a creative brain knows, it really is not that simple; we have to write (or paint, compose music, act, dance, etc.) to clear the mental clutter out of our heads. If we did not, I fear, we would all go stark, raving mad!

So, my advice to any aspiring writer who has happened upon my collection of words here is quite simple…Write!

But do accept that there are no magic shortcuts, no enchanted mice who will finish off your novel in the dead of night while you are tucked up in your bed dreaming of all of the fame and fortune that goes along with being a successful writer… Also, there is very little fame and fortune that goes along with being a successful writer.

Your first attempts may well be not what you'd hoped, the words on the page nothing at all like the fantastic images in your mind's eye, but with slog, blood, sweat, and those ubiquitous tears, you will get there!

MEGAN O'RUSSELL (*Girl of Glass*): Just write. There can be so much pressure when you're first starting out to create something perfect, find a publishing contract, and gain instant success. But loving writing and wanting to jump into being a published author are two different things.

So sit down, write the story you want to tell, and finish the whole project. Then ask yourself if you want to go further. Writing a story is an amazing accomplishment. If you feel satisfied, then you get to be done.

If you read your first draft and decide you really want to be published, then jump into revisions, edits, submission, marketing, and everything else that goes with publication.

But don't let the weight of everything that comes after the first draft come between you and filling the blank page.

ANDREW BUCKLEY (*Hair in All the Wrong Places*): I get asked this a lot, and my answer is lame as hell. It's "keep writing," which sounds like an obvious thing. If you want to be a writer, you should write. It's not always easy, you won't always feel motivated, and sometimes you'll hit a block or you'll have "one of those days." In the end, you just have to keep writing. It's the ones who don't quit that make it in the end.

JOHN BODEN (*Jedi Summer with the Magnetic Kid*): Write honestly. Write what makes you happy/satisfied/content. There is no real template for this gig. What works for you might suck for me. Just do it how you need to. If you're happy with it, and the story has been told the way you want, it's all good.

LAURA ROBERTS (*Haiku for Lovers*): Just write! Whether you're a professional or a hobbyist or have only dreamt of beginning to write, the best thing to do is to sit down and write. Write whatever you want, however you want to write it. Just get it down on paper to begin with. You can edit anything but a blank page, as they say. Some people might tell you it's a waste of time or that you're no good at it, and some of them might even be right, but if it brings you joy to do it, then keep going. If you want to write professionally, write something every day—even if it's just one sentence—and always keep reading. You don't need a degree to be a writer, but you do need to practice and keep learning how to improve and succeed. You don't need a club or community to be a writer, either, but that sometimes helps. Every writer has their own path to get where they're going, so don't worry about what everyone else is doing unless it inspires you. You never know what might work for you, so try everything, and keep track of your results.

ERIN SWEET AL-MEHAIRI (*Breathe, Breathe*): Don't edit while you write—just go with your inspiration, and edit later. Don't overthink your piece on first draft. Read your writing out loud. Find trusted readers for content evaluation. Hire a professional editor with years of experience and training. Don't compete with other authors in turn of output. We all are unique, so don't rush your work to publication. Pull up your big person underwear, and get ready for the ride of your life.

H.R. BOLDWOOD (*The Corpse Whisperer*): Make stretch goals. Challenge yourself by writing a story that you have no idea how to write—a different genre, something that's out of your wheelhouse. I guarantee you will be pleasantly surprised at your efforts if you simply trust the process and let the words fly. Check your ego at the door. Find a solid writing group and a mentor if you can. Be open to the advice you receive. Not all the input will work for you. But chances are, if you hear the same criticism from more than one person, there's probably something to it. At the end of the day, the story is yours. You decide what stays and what goes. Learn from your mistakes. And above all, remember that spell check is simply a tool. It doesn't have a brain, and it won't stop you from using the wrong form of a word. That's why we proofread, proofread, and then proofread again.

JULIA BRAMER (*The Vitamin D Treatment*): Watch the ego. I mean this both positively and negatively. If we rely too much on what others think of our work, seeking to win awards, contests, and publications, it affects the writing, and it kills the muse. We become focused on what *they* want (whomever they happen to be), not on what we are capable of. When we have success on the outside, we begin to churn out more of the same thing, and we take fewer risks in order to keep the success going. When we have challenges and struggle, sometimes the opposite can happen, and we become so defeated that we don't want to try anymore.

When I started writing, I published some poems and stories that today embarrass me. Some of them even won awards. Other works I am still proud of, and some of my best work, in my opinion, is not yet published. About ten years ago, I stopped submitting my work regularly because I found myself caring a little too much about whether or not it was going to be met with validation and praise, which by proxy would mean that *I* was being validated and praised. My entire sense of self-worth was in their hands! I also realized that I was putting my work in the hands of often clueless and uninterested grad students just trying to get a good grade on their MFA literary journal, or to minimum-wage slush pile interns with twenty or more years less experience than I have. These gatekeepers are often looking to publish the current literary trends and topics, or worse, they are looking to publish their friends who will publish them in turn. As I'm in my mid-fifties, there is a very good chance that they will miss themes, nuances, or outright points I'm trying to make, and I'm definitely not going to sound like I'm one of them. It's easier to step outside of the game and build your skills, throwing your best work into the contests and publications that matter when you *know* you have something magical. And then if you are accepted, thank the muse and get back to work, knowing you got lucky. Don't forget that in Greek myth, *Hubris* was the downfall of both gods and man. Those Greeks knew a thing or two.

RANDEE DAWN (*Home for the Holidays*): Keep at it. Writers write. They don't bitch about not being able to or finding time to. They put words on pages, and then they rearrange those words because those first words generally stink. Find fellow writers whose advice and criticism you trust—and know what advice to take, and what you can ignore.

And while you're doing all those things, remember to keep your world busy and open and full of new input—because those are the souls you'll be stealing for the next words you put down on the paper.

LANNY LARCINESE (*I Detest All My Sins*): Don't judge yourself (yet), but write, write, write. You may begin with nothing more than a scene, or a name, or a title, or an incident. Don't worry about quality. Deploy your passion to the learning of craft, an endeavor that must never stop. Join writers groups. We all love to talk writing. Nobody will pull hierarchical bullshit on you. Most writers groups have a mix of people from all points of the experience and accomplishment curve. You will soon learn your worries, problems, and insecurities about your writing are universal. It's a good and inexpensive way to learn craft, the business, and to work out story dilemmas. And it's great group therapy. Happy scribbling!

KATE JONEZ (*Lady Bits*): Spend lots of time learning how to write. After that, learn how to be an entertaining reader and an interesting speaker. It's not good enough to be adequate and keep your hands from shaking. If you're successful as writer, you'll be expected to stand in front of crowds all the time. Your speaking needs to be as entertaining as your writing.

SCOTT M. GORISCAK (*Horrorism*): You need to have a thick skin to be an author; there will be a time where your work will be critiqued or rejected. Take it as a learning experience, not a personal attack. Keep writing.

ADRIENNE DELWO (*Hero Academy*): First, I'd tell them to stop using the phrase "aspiring writer." You don't see someone playing the guitar and call them an aspiring guitarist. If you write, you're a writer. You may aspire to be a professional writer or a successful writer, but you're already a writer. Own it, and don't judge your worth as a writer based on what you've earned or whether you're published.

Second, you can take classes and read books and go to conferences and learn about writing forever, but the best way to become a better writer is to write more. Sure, those other things can help, but writing is the most important. A muscle doesn't get stronger when you read about the best way to exercise it. Write. Then write more.

Third, just accept now that your first draft will be crap. Don't spend forever revising your early scenes to make them perfect because it'll prevent you from ever getting to the end, and until you're at the end, you don't really know the story. Write the whole thing, then make it better.

Finally, no, you cannot edit yourself. Why? Because you know what you meant, so that's how it'll come across to you. Get and accept input from other people, and use it to improve the next draft.

ESSELL PRATT (*Sharkantula*): The best advice I can give is to simply write. Even the worst writings can lead to amazing ideas later. Keep everything in a file, whether it be a poem, story, or even a one-line thought. You never know when you'll be inspired to revisit the idea and make it something much more than it was.

GEORGE LEA (*Strange Playgrounds*): There is nothing worse than hollow or empty writing—writing that exists because the person creating it wants to be acknowledged as a writer. If you don't feel it, don't expect anyone else to. If you're writing something horrific or disturbing, make sure it's exactly that: that it arouses those emotions. If you're writing something erotic, make sure it comes from a place of earnest arousal and desire.

ERIC J. GUIGNARD (*That Which Grows Wild*): Be confident to fail. Read broadly. Experiment. What I tell others, and what I repeat to myself like a mantra, is simply: "Keep writing, and remember that every rejection is an opportunity for improvement!"

MERCEDES M. YARDLEY (*Pretty Little Dead Girls*): Writing and publishing is easier now than it has ever been. The Internet has changed the game completely. You can search for any information you want to know. How do you craft a good story? That info is readily available. How do you find an agent? Easy to look up. You can send the story electronically instead of printing out a giant manuscript and dropping it off at the post office. The world is quite literally at your fingertips. Don't squander the resources you have available. Authors fifty years ago would have killed to have our advantages.

Also, remain professional. You can be a fun person to work with, but get your work done. Don't go off the rails on somebody you have a spat with, etc. I'm horrified at the drama inside the author's community, and it's often over tiny things that aren't important in the grand scheme. The writing community is very small, so don't mark yourself as the writer nobody wants to work with.

ROBERT FORD (*The God Beneath My Garden*): Don't chase what's hot or the audience. Always write for you. What sort of story would you like to read? Because you're going to be spending quite some time with whatever you're working on, and you'd damned well better enjoy it. After Twilight came out, there were dozens of books chasing that hot title. Same with Harry Potter, Fifty Shades of Gray, and you name it. And the new titles all fizzled because the writer was chasing what was hot. They weren't original. Write for you.

C. HOPE CLARK (*Murder on Edisto*): I also don't believe in reading bad work. Just like we read good writing in hope it rubs off on us or some of its lessons and style cling to our writing brain, we avoid bad writing for the same reasons. We don't want those wordings and mistakes finding hidey-holes in our minds. If I pick up a book that isn't resonating with me, or in which I find many mistakes and can easily see the "fast" writing, I put it down unfinished for fear of it infiltrating my work. Surround yourself with good writing. Read way more than you write. Write way more words than you keep. Edit and distill to your best material. Be willing to throw away work and focus on quality. Give yourself permission to take time with your story. But most of all, show up to work daily. Thinking about writing isn't writing. Talking about writing isn't writing. Writing is writing.

W.B.J. WILLIAMS (*The Garden at the Roof of the World*): Three things: don't worry about the market, write what you love, because if you don't love it, no one will. There is no overall correct way to write, find what works for you and do that. Some stories may need an outline and other won't, so don't force an outline unless it helps you.

MARTIN ROSE (*Bring Me Flesh, I'll Bring Hell*): When you look at a map, there's a compass. It's meant to help you navigate, but it's also meant to be a picture of the planet itself. It's meant to help you orient yourself—because if you know where you are in the universe, you also know who you are. If you are living your writing life by what's been published in the last year, and not the last ten years, the last fifty years, the last 100 years, or the last 1,000 years, then you don't know where, or who, you are in the writing field. If you're in it for casual reasons, or you don't care, then it's no big deal because it doesn't matter to you, it doesn't mean you can't grab onto success. Have at it. If you want to make this a career, you might want to get the big picture perspective on writing and how our reading and writing habits have changed across time. It should make you humble—and inspire you to define why you're doing it in the first place. Once you know where you are, you have a greater chance to go farther than where you started.

PEGGY A. WHEELER (*Chaco*): The best advice I ever received was from a talk I attended given by Margaret Atwood: "Don't write what you know. Write what you're passionate about." I cannot imagine that Arthur Golden, who authored *Memoirs of a Geisha*, ever was a Japanese woman, a Geisha who lived in pre-WWII Japan. I doubt Ray Bradbury ever went to Mars or ever met an actual Martian. You get the idea. The trick if you are writing something you don't know is to perform deep research from solid sources and maintain a high level of respect (maybe employ sensitivity reviewers) for your subject matter and characters.

TODD KEISLING (*The Smile Factory*): Temper your expectations, and be sure you're doing it for the right reasons. Writing isn't easy or glamorous or profitable for most, and overall, it's a long game if you want to find any sort of success. Be patient, be tenacious, be honest, and be humble. Goddammit, be humble.

LORI R. LOPEZ (*The Strange Tale of Oddzilla*): Be yourself. Discover your own unique voice. This can take years. Many years. The best advice I could give is to read and practice. Do not imitate. Listen for your natural voice. That is what will make your writing special. That is what will enable it to stand out from everyone who is trying to be like someone else. We are undoubtedly influenced by what we read, watch, hear, and live—by experience and surroundings, our past and our present. Spend time living. Tap into your life. Live other lives through books. Grow as a person.

You may find your work being compared. Take such praise as a compliment, but do not strive to reproduce another style. Your own is waiting for you. Reach in and tug it out, gently, gradually. This can require patience and perseverance. If writing is what you burn to do, what you feel you must do—then your voice is there. It's part of you. Try not to ignore it. And heed the tiny voice that whispers in your ear. It's usually right.

PAUL FLEWITT (*Poor Jeffrey*): First drafts are always shit. They are just you telling yourself the story, so don't worry about it. The story is there when you wipe the shit away.

GIL VALLE (*A Gathering of Evil*): The thought of writing when you're staring at a blank screen on Microsoft Word can be daunting and overwhelming. You might wonder if you can actually put in the necessary amount of focus and work to finish the entire manuscript. I highly recommend not thinking too far down the line. It's a marathon, not a sprint, and some days you are going to feel better about writing than others.

Do your best work on those better days. I don't think it is necessary to adhere to a strict schedule because then it feels like a job, rather than something you want to do. I have found that outlining helps a great deal. You can do a chapter outline, "beginning, middle, and end," or whatever. Just put something down. Have your ending in mind, and then work your way to it. Use the notepad on your smart phone (or an actual notepad), and if you are out somewhere and you think about something for your story, jot it down right away. Those "eureka" moments for something that may be missing can happen at any time, and you don't want to forget any detail.

JESSICA MCHUGH (*Rabbits in the Garden*): Don't forget to have fun. Writing is mentally and emotionally strenuous no matter what, and trying to make a career out of it is more stressful than I can possibly convey. If you're not deriving enjoyment from creating, refining, and growing with your art, you'll burn out really fast. Hell, even if you are enjoying yourself, you might experience burnout, so please be kind to yourself and find the fun where you can.

SCOTT M. BAKER (*Nazi Ghouls from Space*): Write. It doesn't matter if it's good or if you only get down a few hundred words a day. Like any craft, the more you practice, the better you'll get at it. But you have to write every day. I know dozens of wannabe writers who have notebooks filled with plot outlines, character bios, and world developments, yet have never put a single word down on paper. I tell all aspiring writers that if you complete a single page a day, which anyone can accomplish, at the end of a year, you'll have a 365-page book.

J. STEFFY (*Evolution of a Monster*): Don't try setting a pace. Don't make it your job. Enjoy it as a hobby, and it will stay enjoyable. Even a paragraph a day will eventually get you a book.

S.A. COSBY (*My Darkest Prayer*): Get used to the word no, but keep looking for that one yes.

J.C. MICHAEL (*Pandemonium*): Don't rush to self-publish. It's so easy now, and many people will tell you that if you don't find a publisher, don't worry, do it on your own. Sure you can, but be honest, is your story really that good? Is it the best it could be? Once you put something out there, you'll be judged on it, and if you simply ran spellcheck and got a mate to give it the once-over, the chances are it'll be full of mistakes and you'll get a hammering. Same with D.I.Y. covers. It shows. I know it's tempting to self-publish, it's what I did, and like I couldn't, maybe you can't afford an editor and a cover designer, but before you decide that you may as well put it out there as not, just pause for a second and consider this—if it's crap, it won't sell, and your name is your brand, so do you really want to put out a sub-standard product? I was lucky, my "brand" wasn't damaged by publishing on Lulu and selling next to nothing, but that was ten years ago, and if you self-publish now on Amazon, you're a lot more exposed. My other piece of advice is stick with it as there are opportunities out there, and self-publishing has its place, but it isn't a quick and easy option if you're going to do it right.

CHAD LUTZKE (*The Same Deep Water as You*): Other than the obligatory "read books and write as much as you can", trust the reader. Don't spoonfeed, and don't spell everything out. If you've already set a specific tone, that should be enough to carry the scene. We don't need to know every thought inside the narrator's head. This is the kind of thing you show and don't tell. When tempted to tell us how scared a character feels, how alone they are, how angry they are, don't do it. Show us. And careful with descriptions. I've seen a lot of writers using descriptive info dumps. If you need to describe something, do it organically. Don't force it. Do we absolutely have to know what clothes the character has on? Their eye color? Unless it's detrimental to the story, you can never ruin a good story with lack of description. Every one of us has the tendency to create our own pictures in our minds eye without much cueing. Also, stay away from cliches, both in prose and tropes. We know that ex-cops are all practicing alcoholics. Don't beat that dead horse. It's not even worth petting.

EDWARD LEE (*White Trash Gothic*): This is what the late, Fantasy Award-winning novelist Brian McNaughton told me in the early '80s: write a page a day, and in a year, you have a book. You've gotta write every day. It's like push-ups; if you do it every day, you get stronger and more enthusiastic by your progress. If you don't do it every day, it becomes a pain in the ass. There's only one way to be a writer: write!

RHONDA PARRISH (*Fae*): Build a community. This thing we do? It's freaking hard. I'm not sure it's possible to do it alone. I mean, I guess you could, but it'll be a lot less fun, and it'll twist you up like a pretzel. Build a community. They'll keep you going through the dark parts, through the pits and the B.S. And give back to that community. Because writing is a team sport.

RICHARD GODWIN (*Savage Highway*): Read as much as you can, and study what writers do and if it works. Write every day.

BARBARA ELLE (*Death in Vermillion*): Write at your own pace, but always have your goal in mind. Keep pushing forward. Never dismiss an idea out of hand; write it down. You may use it later. Enjoy your own work—my characters are my friends (even if I kill them).

STEPHEN SPIGNESI (*Dialogues*): Unpublished, aspiring writers should understand, first and foremost, that publishing is a business and that books are merchandise. They need to have two heads: artist and marketer.

I do writing workshops at libraries, and what I've learned is that most first-time, unpublished writers have no clue what to do once they've finished writing something. The next steps often require more work than the writing itself.

Anyone can be a writer. You don't have to take a test and get a license like accountants, or welders. Thus, many writers, once they've written something, are stalled at a very early stage of the publishing process because they don't have an agent and have no clue as to how to approach the publishing industry. That's why so many writers self-publish.

I always suggest that writers work diligently to acquire an agent if at all possible. PublishersMarketplace.com has an entire section of Literary Agents looking for clients. They even provide instructions as to how to submit to them.

Breaking into the publishing industry is a daunting task. But it's done every day, and it's always a matter of doing the research and approaching agents and, at some point, editors, professionally and with great respect for their time. And having some well-nurtured talent doesn't hurt, either.

GREG HICKEY (*The Friar's Lantern*): Just write. Don't get bogged down in overanalyzing your work. Don't worry about getting it published right away. Don't tell yourself you'll start your novel in the New Year, during NaNoWriMo or when you have more time. Just start writing now. You don't have to give yourself a word count. Instead, commit to writing every day, whether that's jotting down ideas in a journal, polishing up an old draft, or filling a blank page with everything you can think of.

Sure, it's important to learn about plot, pacing, grammar, character development, and story structure. But the biggest difference between writers and aspiring writers is that writers write, and aspiring writers talk about wanting to write. Most writers are great procrastinators because it's not an easy task to park yourself in front of a computer or a notebook for hours on end. But that's what writing is. If you want to be a writer, that's what you have to do. You can learn as you go. You'll get better with practice. But it always requires a time commitment and work.

M. NAIDOO (*Where Sleeping Lies Lie*): Don't try and make your first draft perfect, or you'll forever be going back to fix sentence after sentence and never finish anything. Let the words flow, and allow yourself to write paragraphs that you're not happy with. Keep moving; you can always go back later and edit the hell out of it. Just get that first draft down on paper, then you'll have something to polish till it shines.

BEN OHMART (*The Rerun of Dracula*): You need a second mind. Preferably someone you don't love, someone you don't owe money to or see every day. Pay them or praise them, but get someone whose opinion you respect and doesn't take forever. As I say, it's a difficult chore. But unless you yourself have that excellent shit-judger, like I think Hemingway said he had, which can only be proven by success, you need at the very least a relentless reader who will tell you the real deal.

B.R. STATEHAM (*Murder Is Our Business*): Grow a thick skin, son. The Nos will far exceed the 'Yeses.' You've got to learn to shake off the negatives and keep plugging away. And you've got to decide on one of two things as a writer. Do you want to be a great writer? Or do you want to be a great story teller. I think the choice is important. In my opinion, unsuccessful writers eventually become discouraged and fade away. But a storyteller never stops telling stories. Never.

DOUGLAS BRODE (*Sweet Prince: The Passion of Hamlet*): You want to write, write, write? First, read, read, read! When you're young, if you are anything like me, you go and imitate what you saw the great writers do. You know, the highest form of flattery. So I wrote A Separate Peace and The Catcher in the Rye. Only problem? Others had already written them and written them better. Don't feel bad...everybody does that. Watch Spielberg's early films—every shot is taken from some classic shot in Hitchcock, Hawks, Ford, Welles, etc. His early movies are pastiches of what he loved while watching movies. Not anymore! "When I became a man, I put aside childish things." While learning from the masters, he then went on to gradually discover his own unique style. That's what makes him great. Peter Bogdanovich never did. That's why he's forgotten as a mere imitator of the great ones. Your style comes slowly and gradually—you do retain things that you learned from others that you read and were influenced by—but now they really are truly influences, not imitations. They have been draw into your own organic style. You kind of see it taking shape and then one day...voila...there it is. You found your voice, which every successful writer must do, just like every successful singer. Finding your muse? FORGET ABOUT IT! Think of yourself as a guy who works in a diner and flips hamburgers on a grill all day. And is good at it—people come to his place because he knows what he is doing, having learned by doing. You do the same thing...only with words on the empty page. His job is to fill up hungry people's empty tummies. Your job: fill up that blank page. Because even if what you turn out isn't the filet mignon of writing, it will—like a solid cheeseburger—get the job done. Next stop? Talking someone into publishing it. When that happens, you are not only a writer...you are a professional.

www.ingramcontent.com/pod-product-compliance
Lightning Source LLC
Chambersburg PA
CBHW051131160426
43195CB00014B/2429